BEING MANKIND

Concept by *Mark Lazarus* & *Darshan Sanghrajka*
Produced by *Super Being Labs*
Producer *Jenny Corrie*
Associate producer & photographer *Priya Dabasia*
Editor *Joe Byrde*

Foreword by *Anthony Joshua*

Brand by *Super Being Labs*
Cover by *Matthew Bateman*
Design by *Abizer Kapadia*
Typeset in *Franklin Gothic URW & Arno Pro*

Made in the UK

Published by *Super Being Labs*, London 2016

ISBN 978-0-9954848-0-1

© Being HumanKind Ltd
London 2016

1st edition 2016

For more information visit *www.beingmankind.org*

BEING MANKIND

Volume 1

CONTENTS

01

02

03

FOREWORD

by **Anthony Joshua MBE**
World Heavyweight Champion

Before a fight I focus on not getting beaten, but I'm never nervous. By training hard every day in the gym I make sure the fight is won before I even step into the ring. Life's all in the preparation. No matter what you achieve, no matter where you are going or where you have been, motivation should never taper down. You have to stay hungry. There are a lot of doors open to you if you're prepared to apply yourself and make the most of what opportunities come your way.

We're lucky enough to live in the modern world with access to so much information. It's easy to find examples of successful people and see what they've been through to get where they are. We have the blueprints of those before us to build our own futures. There are certainly individuals who drive me to be better, but I draw the most inspiration from the world I live in and the place I hold within it. It's important to listen to those older than you, those who have been there and seen it all before. Everyone has a different sense of reality – an animal will know its surroundings through its senses, just as we see our world through our own. I see my world knowing I won't be here forever. We all have an expiry date, that's the reality of life. When I wake up in the morning and look around me, how can I not be inspired? I'm living, breathing, and I'm on this earth.

I've always been respectful, even as a child. I come from a massive community in Watford, where everyone knows everyone else. It's so easy to follow the crowd rather than make your own decisions, and that was the case for me. When I moved away from home I began to isolate myself from certain circles and think independently. As I became more disciplined, I started to reap the benefits in my boxing. It's so important to do what's right for you. I never used to have a strategy for overcoming moments of doubt – I could see others who hadn't achieved half the things I had, yet were more confident than me. By watching them I learned to stop worrying. I simply had to believe in myself and my ability, and that comes with time.

Maintaining a close connection with the GB amateur squad helps keep my feet on the ground. It's easy to get carried away with success, so I deliberately surround myself with other like-minded people. The greatest advice I can give anyone is to be open, be honest, and above all be an individual thinker. My number one value is respect. That's everything to me, that's all I want.

INTRODUCTION

Today there are 3,477,829,638 people who were born male. At some point every one of those will ask themselves what it means to be a man in the world we live in. They'll do this because unfortunately the world *still* defines people by their gender, but these stereotypes create expectations that stand in the way of being a human first. To look at life purely through the lens of old-fashioned masculinity is short-sighted.

After all, you can be powerful but compassionate, strong but weak, competitive but giving, courageous but scared, the provider while being provided for. The list goes on. None of those choices should be defined by your gender, yet the unwritten rules make it seem that they are. These expectations have not only inflicted damage on men, but also on the other 3,946,825,237 people on this earth. We need to help the next generation to understand their roles as individuals, and only then can they start to positively understand their relationships with those around them. To do this, Mark and I felt that rather than look at people as men, we ought to look at men as people.

Jenny and Priya have helped start something that has so much potential. They've not only listened carefully to us but also the hundreds of men they spoke to. Through their diverse experiences we wanted to show that once you get past the gender expectations, you find that the only unbreakable code in humanity is kindness. Hence *Being ManKind* was born. We hope that through the stories told here, men will become the greatest *individuals* they can be, both for themselves and those around them; Society will benefit as a result and most importantly, it will set us on a path to equality, where we all succeed together.

Darshan Sanghrajka
Super Being Labs

Growing up I was lucky enough to have male role models around me to learn from. Some lessons were harder than others, but at least I had the chance to listen. This book will give others the same chance. As my kids grow up, I want to bring to life concepts that are hard to teach but important to tell through stories like these. Jenny, Priya, Darshan and I wanted to capture the human spirit and what it can achieve when it's not confined by stereotypes. We hope this is the beginning. These stories are talking to you, it's the best cheat sheet you will ever have.

Mark Lazarus

On hearing Mark and Darshan's idea, we instantly knew that we wanted to be involved. Like them, we felt it was less important to focus on redefining masculinity and instead to explore what it is to be a good person.

Traditionally, there is a cultural expectation that men should be in control of their emotions at all times. Many equate a loss of control with weakness of character. Discouraging men from expressing their feelings or seeking help may perpetuate that trend. In recent years, there has been an increasing focus on challenging female stereotypes. Through this project, we hope to address the unique issues that men and boys face in the 21st Century.

Being ManKind is the start of a conversation. The book is a collection of inspiring stories told by men from all walks of life. Each is an honest account of their experiences, ranging from the ordinary to the extraordinary. From one man's use of comedy to break the stigma around anorexia, to a paratrooper who lost his legs on the battlefield and now rows for Great Britain. These are not a series of lectures, but an opportunity for young men to draw on the diversity of experiences presented here to decide for themselves what it means to be a man in today's society. In Anthony Joshua's words, "We have the blueprints of those before us to build our own futures".

It has been an absolute pleasure getting to know these incredible people and their stories. We were lucky enough to be able to spend time with each person, and then capture photos that mirrored the beautiful honesty of their accounts.

We are so excited that this book will be the first volume of a larger collection, and the start of a bigger project across the UK and beyond. We were blown away by the number of entries we received, but unfortunately we couldn't include them all in this edition. Our unreserved thanks go out to all those individuals who helped contribute to the project in any form, and to those men who went above and beyond putting their words to paper.

We want these stories to create conversations everywhere, but especially in schools and youth organisations. We want to build a community to make a positive change. We can't achieve this through one book alone, but this is the beginning of something bigger. There is so much more to come.

To get involved with our mission, please get in touch at *www.beingmankind.org*

Jenny Corrie
Producer

Priya Dabasia
Associate Producer & Photographer

01

No Limits

01 UNCONQUERABLE
Scott Meenagh

I grew up in Cumbernauld, just outside Glasgow. It was quite a rough area with a lot of distractions. I wasn't massively engaged in school – not a troublemaker, I just found it hard to find a focus. But I always, always wanted to be a soldier.

At school, rugby kept me on the straight and narrow. Most of the guys I hung out with ended up in jail. It could have gone either way for me, but having the discipline of playing for the club, going out on that pitch every Sunday and knocking lumps out of somebody was the only thing that kept me sane.

At 16 I joined the army at the Foundation College in Harrogate. That's where I really started coming into my own. Adults treated us as adults, and I thrived. From amounting to nothing at school, I went to the top of my class. I turned a huge corner there, and left a Junior Corporal. But after a year and a half I picked up a shoulder injury and was immediately discharged. My career was over. I had signed up for the job of my dreams and was loving life, I didn't have a plan B. I was 17, back in Cumbernauld, and on the dole.

It's funny how you have those moments, those conversations that change everything. I'd gone off the rails a bit. After waking one morning with a terrible hangover, a friend asked me if I wanted to play rugby with his team in Edinburgh. I played a decent first game, and as I came off the park a guy approached me. He was running a training camp in France for three weeks. A couple of players had dropped out; did I want to come? I phoned to quit my job there and then.

Playing rugby at a national level again gave me some real drive. With renewed purpose, I reapplied for the army. I fought my corner for 18 months, travelling all over the country to see different surgeons. I did as many press-ups as I could physically stand in the surgeon's office to show how strong my shoulder was. He gave me a chance, and I was signed off to join the Parachute Regiment in May 2009.

It's the hardest regiment. I spent the next seven months training in absolute hell. There were some really difficult moments, but it was more my body giving up, never my mind. My grandfather, who was a huge influence in my life, was terminally ill at the time. After my passing out parade, one of my proudest moments was going home to him in my uniform. On 25th January, Burns Night, he finally passed away.

A year to the day of his death, I was involved in an incident that would alter the course of my life again. Two halves of the patrol were out in Afghanistan, going north under the cover of darkness so as to catch the Taliban when it lifted. While getting into position, one of the lads, Liam, stepped on an IED (improvised explosive device) and lost both his legs.

Securing the area to provide cover for the helicopters, it soon became clear that this had become a recovery operation. We had to find Liam's kit and weapon in the dark. We found other things. Parts of Liam's equipment, parts of Liam. Just as we were leaving, we noticed his metal detector was missing and had to go back in. That's when my friend, Martin Bell, and I walked onto the track. He said, "We've seen enough, this is getting too dangerous". As I turned around, I breathed a deep sigh of relief. We didn't have to search any further, we could go back the way we came. I took two steps and everything went black.

It was like being tackled and punched in the face at the same time. I knew what had happened before it had even detonated. When I found myself on my back, unable to move, I thought, "I'm dead, I can't believe I've gone and died". As my poor mum mourned the anniversary of her father's death, she was going to get that knock on the door. My world passed in slow motion, my ears were ringing. Then all of a sudden, everything came rushing back. I looked up and saw a big, beautiful, blue sky and the sound of everyone shouting around me. As I came to, I started putting tourniquets on my legs to stop the bleeding. Five paratroopers circled in and put me on a stretcher. The boys had got me, I was going home.

Another explosion.

Martin Bell had stepped on another IED and he was cut in half. It killed him instantly and wounded everyone else on the stretcher. Two lads were still *compos mentis*, despite suffering severe burns and injuries. Gavin had been totally blinded, but he kept his hand on the stretcher and dragged me out of the minefield. It was the bravest thing I've ever seen. They got me back, and five of us went up in a helicopter to Camp Bastion where I received life-saving surgery. Within six hours of being wounded, I was back in the UK.

I woke up from an induced coma to see my mum and dad standing in front of me. It was a huge relief to be home. I would spend the next four months in hospital. As well as losing both legs, I needed significant reconstructive surgery to repair the many internal and external injuries I had sustained. It was a pretty hard time. My world had been turned upside down. I'd gone from being as fit and capable as a human being can be, to having somebody brush my teeth and roll me over to wash me. I was never going to be a rugby player or a soldier again. I had to start looking for a new playing field.

I gave myself short-term goals to achieve: getting out of bed, getting into the wheelchair, getting to the end of the corridor. When I got there, I was so exhausted my mum had to push me back. I tested my limits every day. When I got to Headley Court Rehabilitation Centre, I made walking a priority. I didn't want to stay in a wheelchair, so I was damned focused. The day I got my test sockets, I pushed my wheelchair to the other side of the room. These were my legs now.

I started off on stubbies. They're like small, tin legs, and the minute I got them I insisted on walking everywhere. I wasn't going to use my stick. I got to Headley Court on a Wednesday and I was walking on stubbies by the Friday morning. I'm pretty stubborn.

For the next year I made rehab my absolute goal. I would pick somebody who was at a place in recovery where I wanted to be, and paint a target on their back. I'd spend however long it took me to come to their level and then find myself surpassing them. I'd be on my legs and I'd think, I've learned to walk so I need to learn to run, I'm going to walk on different surfaces, now I'm going to climb. I became really competitive, but that was good for me.

A quote we always used in the regiment is, "Paratroopers never take the easy option". So in rehab I thought, never make it easy for yourself, do something no one else is doing. I learned by doing and trying and failing.

Sport was really important to my recovery. I got into rowing by chance. I had a colostomy bag because of the internal injuries, and I needed to lose some weight around my stomach for the surgery to have it reversed. I had a spare weekend in London and was staying with my mate Kingsley, who had lost three limbs in the war. I received an email about a rowing development camp there and thought, why not?

Rowing up and down the docks in London humbled me. It buried me. I realised I wasn't the guy I used to be. But actually, by putting myself in a new hole, the feeling of confidence it gave me lifted me to another level. I didn't care what it took, I wanted to train full time.

Coached voluntarily by my mate John Blair, we trained seven days a week for 18 months, focusing everything on making the Great Britain rowing team. After my performance at the Invictus Games selection, I made the selection for Team GB that December.

Rowing was a game changer for me. It has restored in me the infectious optimism I had as a paratrooper. It saved my life and redefined me as an athlete. I would like to think I'm no longer known as a wounded soldier. For a long time I was labelled by the media as the boy who Martin Bell saved. Martin Bell put his life on the line and saved Scott Meenagh, how does it feel being alive while your friend is dead? How does it feel being the guy who lost his legs? I don't want to be known as that. I want people to know me as a developing Great Britain athlete who is punching his weight on the world stage.

It's been a crazy few years and not without dark days, but you have to find coping strategies that work for you. Peaks and troughs are always going to happen. It's about keeping the troughs shallow and short, and knowing how to pull yourself out of them, switch fire and refocus. I've got a lot to be grateful for. I've got a lot of amazing people around me in life – mentors and role models, people who don't even know the influence they've had. Some have changed my life forever. I like to put targets on people's backs who I think are good, and try to surround myself with those who give positive energy.

02 WHEELS OF FORTUNE
Nadenh Poan

Two years after I was born I contracted polio. My parents didn't understand what was wrong with me at first. Cambodia is a developing country and there wasn't much medical information available. Despite hospital intervention, my legs grew progressively weaker until I was finally diagnosed a year later. By this point it was too late for me to walk.

When I started school at six years old, I looked so different from all of the other children. I didn't have a wheelchair, so I had to pull myself along using my hands. My classmates did impressions of me. Running around me in circles, they'd ask, "Nadenh, you've got two legs, why can't you walk?" I was so lonely. My parents tried to push me to go back to school, but I left when I was seven to live on a boat with my dad instead.

He was a fisherman, and we spent most of our time on the river. Over the next few years my dad built me a special canoe and taught me how to swim. I loved living on that boat. In the mornings I would wake up to natural sunlight, the sound of birds, and watch monkeys jumping from one tree to the next. Back in my village I felt like I was separate from everything, but in the jungle I had my own little world.

We returned to land for the Pchum Ben festival when I was 14 years old. Everyone in Cambodia has the day off and cooks delicious food. During the celebrations, a Catholic priest from Spain came down to our village. He asked me why I didn't have a wheelchair. My family couldn't afford one. He explained that in Phnom Penh City there was an organisation that gave wheelchairs to disabled people for free. He offered to take me to the city and give me a wheelchair to help me get around more easily. I had never felt so happy!

I left home that year and went to the hospital. They asked me if I'd like to learn how to walk. I couldn't believe it was possible. At that time my right leg was stuck at an angle so I couldn't straighten it out. I was frightened by the prospect of corrective

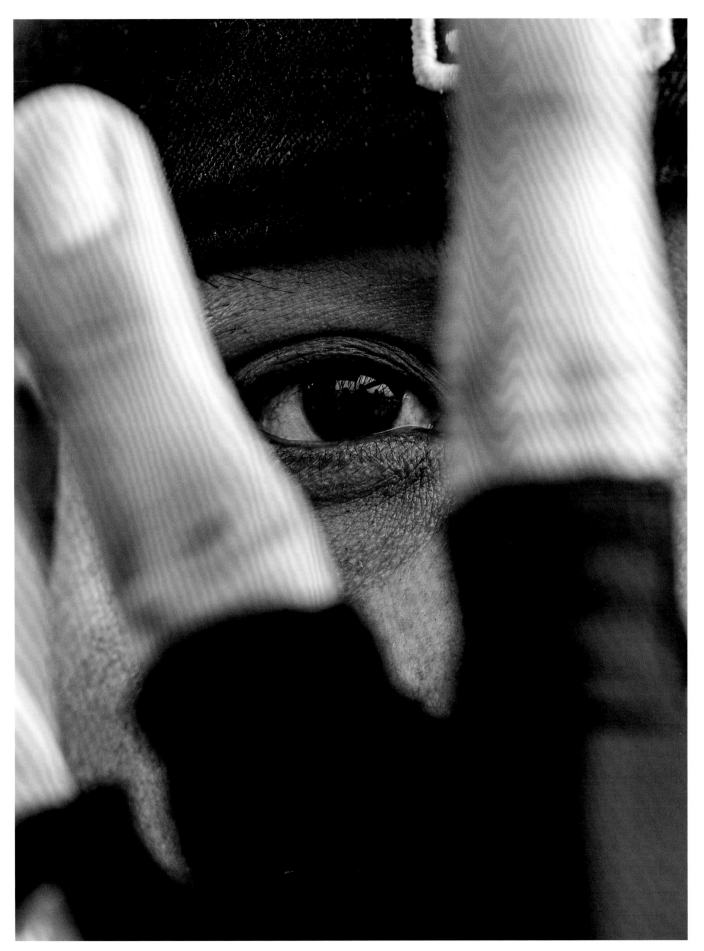

surgery, but after the operation I was able to see my real height for the first time. When I saw my straight legs in the mirror, I looked like a robot! After walking with crutches for six months, I tried without them. It was a revelation.

I was a new person, but after my experience at school I was still unable to read or write. A gentleman who worked for the priest introduced me to the Lavalla School for disabled children in Takhmao City. I saw lots of different people with different disabilities – it made me feel secure, so I decided to stay. I was a 15-year-old boy in a class surrounded by small children, but I didn't care. I was so hungry to learn.

In 2004 a lady called Katie Goald came to the school from the UK to lead a contemporary dance workshop. I found that I really enjoyed dancing – everything I did during that week made me feel free, everything was from my heart. I could do anything I wanted.

In 2005 I joined a new public school, unafraid. Later that year Katie got in touch again. She was putting on a big production and needed a wheelchair dancer. My schedule became taken over by schoolwork and dance training, but it was all worth it. I invited my family and all of my friends to the show. When it was over, my parents came to me and cried. It was so emotional.

From that moment on, I knew this was what I wanted to do with my life.

We toured around many Asian countries – Thailand, Vietnam, Laos, Hong Kong, Indonesia and Singapore. By the time the production ended in 2008 I was at high school and needed money to support my studies. I rang Katie and asked if she had any jobs for me. She offered me some office work in a new production company she had set up, and I moved schools to join her in Kampot.

I was invited to be one of 12 students to train on a two-year course in contemporary dance. On graduation, the company travelled around the UK on a one-month tour. It was here that I attended a summer school developing my dance skills with Stopgap Dance Company. I was entranced – it became my dream to work with them again. I had to apply for a visa three times before I was finally granted to stay in the UK to join their trainee dancer programme. I have since graduated to become part of Stopgap's main touring team.

When I look back at my early life in Cambodia, so much has changed. When I return to my village I'm a bit famous, my peers have seen me on television. People circle around me for a different reason now.

03 A SMALL STEP FOR MAN

Mark Pollock

It's in my nature to take on new challenges. Unbroken by blindness in 1998, I went on to compete in ultra endurance races across deserts, mountains, and the polar ice caps. I always tried to push my limits – I was the first blind person to race to the South Pole in 2009.

In preparation for my expedition to Antarctica, I had taken my lead from the polar explorers who carved those first trails into the Antarctic ice – Shackleton, Scott and Amundsen. They were the pioneers. That was their privilege, their courage, their risk. They charted the unknown world, showing the way for the rest of us 100 years on.

In 2010, a fall from a second-storey window left me paralysed. Spinal cord injury strikes at the very heart of what it means to be human. It turns us from our upright, standing, running, jumping forms into seated compromises of our former selves. It's not just the lack of movement and feeling, it interferes with the body's internal systems that are designed to keep us alive. Multiple infections, nerve pain and uncontrollable spasms are common. These are the things that exhaust even the most determined, that exclude seven out of ten from the workforce, and that leave four of those living under the poverty line.

Despite all of the problems, it is nothing short of a miracle that the formal medical system has released spinal cord injury from the death sentence it used to be. The challenge is that I, like so many, do not want to live the rest of my life in a wheelchair. Up to this point in history it has proven impossible to find a cure for paralysis. But history is filled with accounts of the impossible made possible through human endeavour. The same human endeavour that allowed explorers to reach the South Pole and saw astronauts travel to the moon.

Inspired by those stories of exploration, I began searching for a new wave of pioneers around the world. Innovators working in the field of exercise physiology to maximise what remains intact; robotic engineers creating exoskeletons to help people

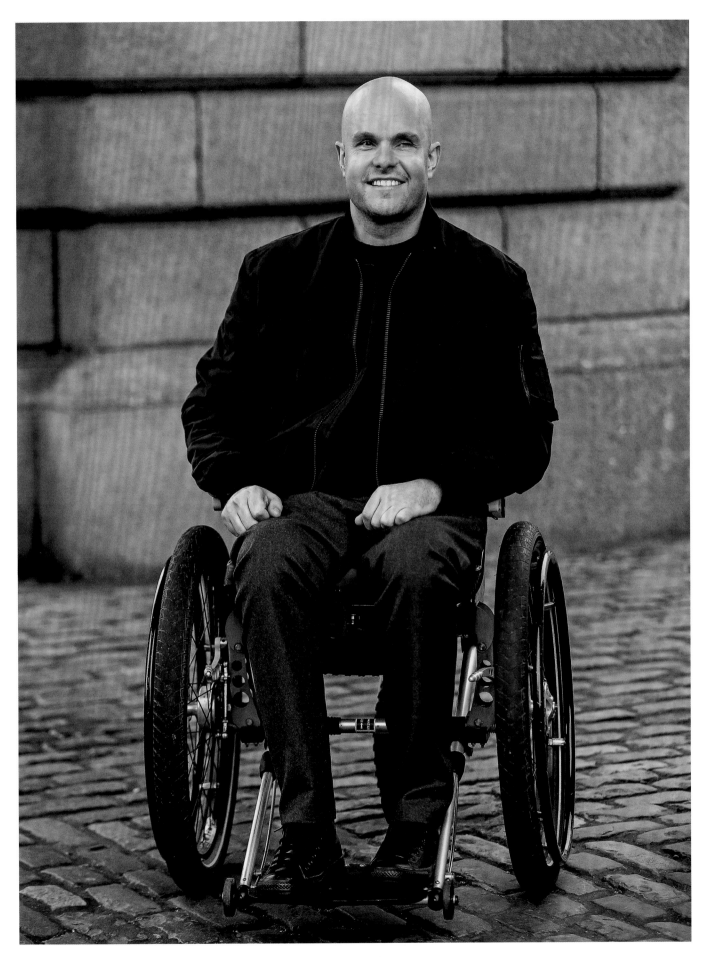

like me stand and walk; and neuroscientists attempting to reignite the nervous system using electrical stimulation of the spinal cord.

Part of a global tour in the summer of 2013 found my fiancée and me sitting in Professor Reggie Edgerton's lab at UCLA in Los Angeles, listening to him describe how he and his collaborator Professor Yury Gerasimenko were working on a new method. Very quickly we proposed that they should combine their research in spinal stimulation with my paralysed legs and their robotic exoskeleton. Within six months we were in LA, exploring new frontiers of research with Nathan Harding, Founder of Ekso Bionics. The result was that I was able to stand and walk, voluntarily assisting the robot while stepping. With the stimulation on my spine supercharging my nervous system, my leg muscles did more and the robot's motors did less.

As their leading test pilot, I've walked hundreds of thousands of steps. But like any other expedition, the research will only continue if we can raise the finances to make it happen. That's why, at the Mark Pollock Trust, we have built a social enterprise to fund our work.

Now, as darkness falls on one night each November, 25,000 people around the world get up from their armchairs and televisions, pull on their running shoes, slip on their red flashing armbands, and hit the road to Run in the Dark. In over 50 cities worldwide these people light up the night, flowing through the streets like lava. Together they are on a mission to fast-track a cure for paralysis on a global scale. People run or walk 5 or 10km at an official event in Dublin, Cork, Belfast, Manchester or London. Or they join one of the 45 pop-up events that take place across six continents from the South Pacific to Northern America.

Sometimes we choose our own challenges; spinal cord injury is one of those challenges that chooses us. It's what we decide to do about it that counts.

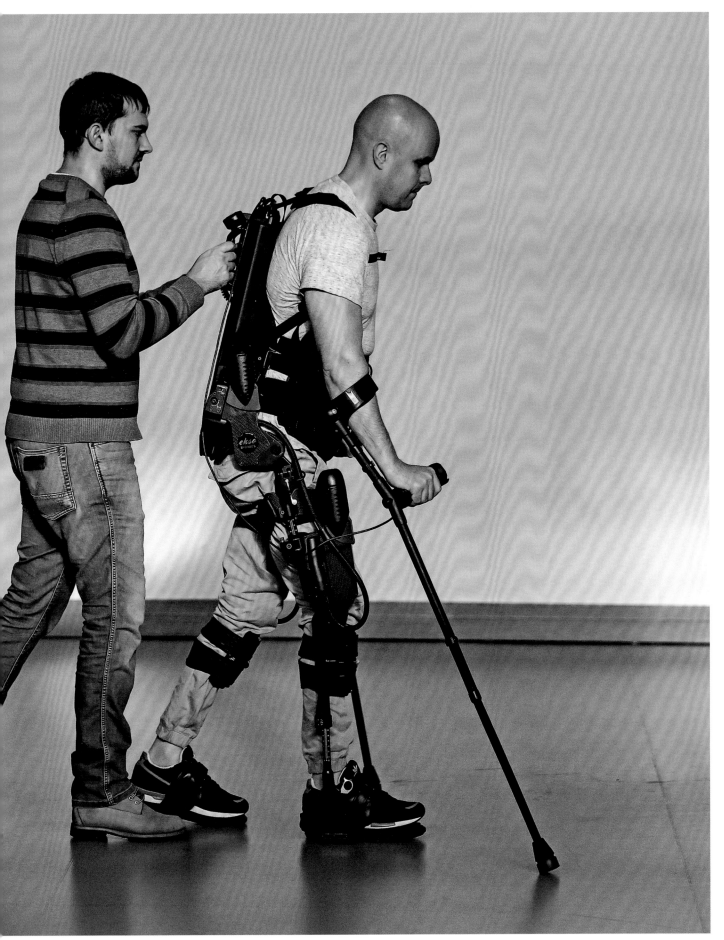

04 DESERT STORM

Mike Fetherstone

The Marathon des Sables is a multi-day ultra-marathon run over six days and 156 miles. From the moment I saw it I was hooked. Sitting down with a glass of wine one evening, browsing the internet, I signed up there and then without telling anyone, not even my wife.

The training regime is brutal. Because I was a 54-year-old fat blob weighing in at over 13 stone, I started nine months ahead to prepare myself. You have to exercise every day for upper body strength, and run five or six times a week, covering up to 80 miles. There are a lot of back-to-backs – 20 miles on one day, followed by another 20 the next – to get your body used to running when it's tired, weak and injured.

When it's pissing down in the depths of winter and the last thing you want to do is get out of bed at four in the morning, it's often hard to stay motivated. But everybody has their own story, everybody has a reason for taking it on. My father had died a year or so beforehand, and that helped give me an extra drive. In the dark moments of the desert – and there were plenty, believe me – I would try to think of him and his fight against cancer.

The desert isn't how you'd imagine it. Thirty percent of it is pure sand, but there are also hills and mountains higher than Snowdon that you've got to climb. You're totally self-supported. You have to take food for the whole week on your back, your feet are absolutely buggered, they're blistered to hell and your shoulders are screaming at you to stop. It's such a relief to get back to your tent at the end of the day. The MdS is described as the Toughest Footrace on Earth, but the reality is you actually walk more than you run. It's physically impossible when it's 50 degrees centigrade, when you've got nine kilograms of pack on your back and your skin is just coming off in lumps. It's 90% strength of mind, 10% body. The pain from your feet is so great at times that only your mind will get you through it. For three quarters of an hour one day, all I said to myself as I ran was, "I

cannot feel this pain, I cannot feel this pain, I cannot feel this pain". You can actually convince yourself. Your mind is so much stronger than your body.

Trudging through the night, having started at ten in the morning and having run for 20 hours, there are some pretty low moments. When it's pitch black in the Sahara Desert, you have no idea where you are, all you want to do is go to sleep. But you have to just keep plodding on.

The experience was described to me as a 'life washer', and it's absolutely true. When you're out there the only things that matter are going to the loo, eating, drinking and sleeping. You come across little kids in the middle of the desert who've got nothing – it teaches you that a lot of what we get caught up in is a total waste of time, it makes you realise what really matters.

05 A LONG WALK FOR FREEDOM

Matthew McVarish

My uncle once said, "Don't tell anyone", but many years later I was really struggling – depressed, confused about my sexuality, and contemplating suicide. I had never spoken about what he used to do to me, and he was still working as a school teacher, running football teams for young boys. I suddenly realised that my silence was dangerous. I was allowing him to continue.

Every fifth person has been sexually abused in their childhood, and if we don't talk about this now then each new generation of children will remain at risk.

When I decided to walk 10,000 miles and encourage every EU government to abolish the law that stops victims of childhood sexual abuse from pressing charges, it seemed impossible. I've now walked 10,000 miles and the Council of Europe are currently meeting to discuss encouraging abolition across all 47 member countries. This one change would allow potentially hundreds of millions of people to achieve justice against their offenders, but when I started this journey I was just trying to stop one.

Sometimes, after my uncle had sexually abused me, he would take me to see a movie. Perhaps it was to help me forget what he had just done; perhaps it was to help him forget. One such night, when I was eleven, he took me to see *Forrest Gump*. As Forrest ran across America, he passed through countless towns, always rushed by journalists asking him why. This stuck with me.

On 31st May 2013, I left London on foot and set out to visit every capital city in the European Union. My plan was simple. Trek 30 miles each day until I had walked all the way around Europe. Sure enough, reporters began to approach me, asking why. By the time I reached the finish line in February 2015, I had spoken on television and radio broadcasted to hundreds of millions of people, and to newspapers translated into thirty

languages. In many countries, I was the first male survivor ever to speak publicly about being sexually abused in childhood, but my walk was more than just an awareness campaign. When I arrived at each city, I asked their government to remove their Statute of Limitations – a time limit that restricts victims from reporting their offender to the police, leaving dangerous criminals free to repeat their crimes.

Within three days of talking to an MP in Bratislava, the Slovakian Parliament launched a motion to discuss abolition of their limitation. Nine months after walking through Hungary, they voted to abolish theirs. Not every country let me speak, but among those who did, the walk catalysed new discussion. It was then that something awesome started happening.

Walking through Italy, I was invited to the Vatican to speak with Pope Francis. Walking through France, I was invited to Strasbourg to speak to the Council of Europe, where every European Government meet in one big room. Walking across the Alps, I was invited to Geneva to speak at the United Nations, where the entire world's leaders come together. When I finally reached Edinburgh, I was joined for the last mile by my entire family and over a thousand supporters from all over the world, while my uncle sat in prison.

The day I decided to take that first step, I didn't know anything about international child protective legislation, and I'd never walked for more than a few hours around the shops. I was just a guy who wanted something to change. I don't believe there's anything special about me, but if there is, it's because there's something special about everyone.

I'm now sitting in Bangkok, invited here to advise on a new global campaign to end child sexual abuse. I never imagined all this when I started. These days, I only walk from the taxi to the aeroplane, but I discovered a new kind of truth on my journey.

The truth is: you can. Whatever the thing is that you tell yourself you can't do, I promise you that you can. You are everything you need to be right now, and everything else will come to you once you start. So go for it, now, today, just start. As Nelson Mandela once said, "It always seems impossible until it's done."

02

Growing Pains

Ojuelegba

I wrote this because they said I shouldn't.

I started to think I couldn't.

But that would let my fam down, and I swore I wouldn't.

Because they taught me that I can do anything I put my mind to,
if your heart is pure, God will guide you.
Make a way, then shine the light too.

See the 'ends' works the same.
You may not need religion, but faith!

I was born in a place called Delta State,
before I flew over to be raised on these estates.

Two different states
but the same things at stake.

We play our chips on the system's roulette table, hoping to catch up.

But the game's fixed so many struggle to stay in the black,
trying to make ends meet.

See,
back home your neighbours are family, and in the hood you're raised as a family;
generations of families, stand as one.

And these politicians we trust none.

If one person can afford to eat a king's meal,
He breaks bread.
That's the way our minds are bred:
Everybody mouth gets fed!

But to make it out, bring ins aren't enough,
it's hard work and luck.

So from young,
my brothers never walked under ladders and pillars. But many

06 POETRY IN MOTION *Emmanuel Speaks*

fell through the cracks, we tried not to step on because the gap was too large.

I wanna break glass ceilings apart, not mirrors.

I wonder, because

'Superstition ain't the way', and I'm trying to make a way in so clear the path for me.

Make proud those that looked after me.

I acknowledge where we've come from.

Seen my Grandfather hunt with a shotgun,

Walked miles to reach the market with my mum's mum.

That's the turf of resilience, and hard work!

This passion comes from deep within,
now we're here to win!

That's what I'm flagging.

The green-white-green boasts natural resources and peace,
so I use my talent and resource to help put minds at ease.

I'm inspired by the Motherland when I dream about the future with my brothers and,

You could ask me every day if I feel I've done enough,

I'll say no!

My G, I got other plans.

I will never stop dreaming until I'm at the top with the whole team in,
smiling and eating!

That's da-vision I wanna multiply when I speak,
trust me it adds up.

Let me teach, not preach,
to each and every ear that wants to listen.
We can make fire from the stick we're given!

This is a warning, I'm heading for your spot, my brother!
My aim is beyond counting figures.
I promise you my heart is bigger,
my God is greater.
I've had my inner G since younger,
I get my energy from hunger.

London to Ojuelegba.
I just wanna see my people living better.

07 GOODFELLA

Daniel Barnes

As a young teenager growing up in South London, I found the attraction of gang culture very appealing. It seemed more like a family and, since I was being raised by my mother and an older sister, the absence of any positive male role models in my life had left a huge negative impact on me. So the gang became my source of belonging, and the gang elders took the place of our fathers.

As the years went on, the gang way became my normality – from earning money through criminal activities, to days out at the theme park and heavy partying. The thought never occurred to me to change my way of life. Even after two years in prison at 16 years old, I just accepted my lifestyle and planned on being wiser and smarter in the future. I didn't think that university or work was for people like me. The rap music we listened to for hours on end glorified drug dealing, murder and criminality. After years of listening to that, you start believing in it and trying to live it out. On the face of it, rap music sells you a dream of fast cars and big houses, but in reality it delivers a nightmare of death, pain and misery.

When I reached 20, the violence had increased to the point that being witness to a stabbing or a shooting was common. In the space of 14 months, three of my closest friends had been murdered by gun crime. But even this didn't make me reassess my life. I couldn't see any way of changing – I thought I would carry on until I was killed or locked up for life.

As time went on, I realised that I had grown up too quickly and had witnessed things that most people hadn't at my age. My childhood and innocence had been robbed by the streets. Becoming consumed by the constant fear of my inevitable death or imprisonment, I travelled outside the UK to rethink how to live my life. I simply asked myself, do I want an early grave or a prison cell? The answer was no.

The next step was to find good people who could help me to identify my skills and interests, which led me to discover that I had leadership potential. I decided to become my own boss and start my own business. After months of planning and research, I opened up a removals and storage company called All in All Removals. It was hard going in the beginning, but I was able to enjoy the simple fact that I was finding peace in my life. Fast forward three years and the company has gone from strength to strength, having a positive impact on active gang members who feel unable to turn their lives around.

We can all strive to better ourselves; we all have the power to shape our futures for the better. I am my own man now, with no more reason to feel unsafe or at risk from anyone.

08 MASQUERADE
Mubarak Mohamud

I was born in Nairobi, Kenya. My dad was an ambassador and we lived in a large house, we had maids and everything. When I was seven we moved to Camden, and I've lived here ever since. I'm the definition of a homeboy. I work here, I live here, I party here.

I got chucked out of school in Year Three for doing stupid things, like bringing in a pellet gun or being disrespectful to teachers. My next school couldn't handle me for a full day, so I was made to do half days. This was soon reduced to quarter days. I was going into school at 9am and leaving at 11.30am every day. The school told my mum that either I had to go to a Pupil Referral Unit or I would be expelled. I ended up going to the unit in Year 8, so I only lasted a year in secondary school. That's when I started bunking off to sell drugs.

All you have to do is stand in Camden and act like a drug dealer, then customers will come to you like crazy. It was a character that I would play every day. I was putting on a mask when I left the house and would only take it off when I came home. I was trying to be someone I wasn't, in search of gratification. Everyone's chasing ratings, and many young people are getting it from gang affiliation. The more drugs you sell, the more ratings you get. It was easy money. For eight years it was like being in a coma because I learned nothing. But in every negative situation, there's got to be a positive. Mine was that I had selling skills. And that's what I always tell the guys who want to work in my shop.

It wasn't until I turned 21 that I really woke up and began to rewire the way I think. It's hard, but it is possible. It's not like the Italian Mafia where people cut your fingers off for leaving the gang. That's fiction. The reality is that people are happy for you, and taking that difficult first step only encourages others to do the same.

You hear the same things, "If you get a criminal record then it's over, you're doomed". Nobody else was going to give me

a job, so I gave one to myself. And not only me, but hopefully thousands of other youngsters in the future. People are often judged by pieces of paper, whereas I look for loyalty and dependability. You don't need to be in education to educate yourself. Your mind is like a recorder – if you fill it up with junk, then that's what it's going to be.

It takes a lot of time to rewire someone's brain, but taking education out of the classroom setting really works for those who've had a bad time at school. I use my theatre background to create a character for them to play. They have to put the mask on, because being polite is seen as alien to them and they don't want to lose their street cred. When they come into work, they come in as that person. You can only change your behaviour by repetition, and this is a repetitive job.

Telling their story to other people allows these young people to move away from the past, because they receive positive encouragement from customers. They've been looking up to the same people I used to – the guys with the big cars, the drugs, the girls – and that's the wrong image. I'm trying to create a good role model. There's a misconception about selling drugs and making a lot of money. In reality, the more money you make, the more money you want – you become greedy. I'm not trying to make easy money. You will never be satisfied unless you make something yourself.

Clime-it Brothers is now in its second year and things are going

well. We've done another two successful festivals, the range has grown, and we've secured a second shop. I want to be a trendsetter for other businesses. You don't have to be a charity to do something good for the community or the environment. If this becomes a successful model, I'd be really happy for other businesses to replicate it. If there was one of these shops in every area, you'd have young people doing something, owning something, having a sense of belonging and taking responsibility. If I can help these guys to help themselves, they can go on to do other things.

We have many success stories. A lot of young people have come here with no experience and then left to find work. It's a big achievement for guys who were previously written off by society. Drug dealing is quick money – you sell the drugs, you get the money. This type of work isn't. You work a whole month and get paid at the end. It's going to take a while to convince some people, but I'm not going to be disheartened if they don't respect what we're trying to do.

Overcoming drug culture has been my biggest challenge. Nevertheless, I'm glad I made that journey. It's taught me what it means to be a man. To me, being a man is to be kind, respectful and about stepping up to responsibility rather than running away from it. I have learned not to look at what's in the next man's pocket. To me, success is preparation meeting opportunity, and I believe that opportunities are out there for everyone.

09 KNOW THYSELF
Jhanai Lelitte

Secondary school is tricky because you just want to be accepted. I managed to get through it by learning how to play the game – how to be in with the crowd but not part of it, to get my work done while they messed about. It was a hard balance to find. They weren't really my friends as such, but there was a respect between us. I spoke to them, but we didn't hang out after school. I'm sure many of them are in prison now.

Schools would hit other schools. Twenty of the strongest lads would go out to neutral ground to clash with those from another district, hyped up and full of adrenaline. I was a big guy, so I was encouraged to make up the numbers. I went along to one, but before we started I saw the police had already arrived. That didn't stop everyone else, but I was able to make up an excuse and slip away unnoticed. I tried to stay on the right side of the law. When I was a witness to someone being stabbed with a bottle, the police came to me for the story because I was the only one with no record. I was proud of that. It was never easy – I was under a lot of pressure to get involved. If I'd refused, I would have been ostracised by my peers and lost the respect I'd built up.

It took some nerve to stay out of it, but I wasn't afraid to say no. I was strong-minded, I knew right from wrong. My dad reminded me that I wouldn't be with these people for the rest of my life, I didn't have to impress them. But you've still got to avoid being a target, and a good way is to deflect the attention elsewhere. Having other interests outside school meant that I was able to keep my own life to myself. I wasn't just sitting indoors waiting for a knock on the door to hang out every evening or waste my weekends.

I wasn't perfect; I got a few detentions. But I was only ever given internal exclusions, where you were isolated from your mates and accompanied to the canteen by a teacher as though it was your last meal on death row. When I was a teenager I was living with just my mum, and there were certain things

she couldn't understand, so I dealt with them on my own. On her birthday one year, I was one warning away from a full exclusion. A guy at school started on me, but I didn't retaliate. I didn't want to bring that sort of news back home as a present. The problem was, he thought he'd got one up on me. A few days later I fought him – it was important to show I couldn't be walked over. My mum never understood why, but that was the way to survive. In life you've got to walk with your chest out.

I worked hard at secondary school, but I lost focus on my studies in sixth form and didn't do well in my exams. I'll never forget the feeling of being unable to answer any of the questions, and I told myself I would never experience that again. I take full responsibility for getting bad marks, but it was impossible not to be influenced by my surroundings at the time.

The school offered me the chance to retake the year, but I needed to make a fresh start away from the same people. Sometimes the most accessible options aren't always best for you. Change can be good. I often thought about my mum and how she had made the decision to move from Brazil to the UK aged 17. I too felt that I needed to venture out and try something new. I started at a new college in Hammersmith, made new friends, and passed my exams.

I try to be philosophical about life. When something 'bad' happens, I look for the reason – there's a positive to be discovered in every situation if you're prepared to change your perspective. When I have kids I'll make sure I'm there for them, available to listen and give advice. Some people think that men don't have any emotions, but we experience the same feelings as women. I do, and every other guy does. I think it's important to channel these emotions into something constructive and not be afraid of how others may react.

I always look to other people who are where I want to be and doing what I want to do, especially if they have a similar background to me. It gives me a better insight into how to get there. Members of my family are great role models, but if I just took my lead from them I'd feel I was narrowing my mind and options. A personality trait I admire in other people is persistence. It's very easy to give up on something if it doesn't work straight away and you experience setbacks. If you keep trying, things will eventually work out.

My step-brother is going to be a dad soon, so I've been thinking about what lessons I'd like to pass on to my niece or nephew. I would tell them not to follow what everyone else is doing but to have their own mindset. It's important to stay true to your own opinions and views. It's important to know yourself.

10 BREAKING THE HABIT
Karl Lokko

My addiction almost destroyed my life. It saw me underachieve in school, it distorted my moral compass, it resulted in the deaths of many of my peers, and the list goes on. You've probably put me in the bracket of a former drug addict, or an alcoholic. But my addiction was to gang culture, and like so many addictions it started out as nothing more than a recreational pastime, a way to socialise with other boys.

By 18, I was addicted to the lifestyle of being a gangster. The money, the power and the status it gave me on my estate in Brixton. The downside was that I'd been shot at more times than I'd had birthdays, I'd been cut on my face, almost blinded, and butchered in my back. I was living life with a pool of negative ambition perverting my potential. My prospects were getting bleaker and bleaker, until a courageous woman on my estate, whose son was also a member of my gang, opened her home to me and several others who were caught in the net.

Her name was Pastor Mimi and she ran a local church in the area. She never condemned us. She acknowledged that we were lost children who needed direction. Her home became our refuge; she would engage with us, counsel us, and help us to identify that our true enemy was not our rivals from another estate but the ideology we followed. This didn't happen overnight. It took time, effort, love and a strategy. She sparked a small flame of change in us that she fanned over a two-year period by challenging and dethroning the notion of gangsterism in our minds. The six of us who lived in the house have all been reformed. We're now trying to help others in our community who are where we've been. In doing so, we're becoming assets, not liabilities, to society.

So much taxpayer money is used to incarcerate youths convicted of gang-related crimes. But prison is not the solution. A fraction of the taxpayer money spent on detaining young people could be used instead to set up a centre to rehabilitate them by mirroring the process I underwent under Pastor Mimi's roof.

03

Lost and Found

11 BITTERSWEET SYMPHONY

Rich Smith

It was the Easter of my first year at university that I received the worst phone call of my life.

After college I had been completely lost and didn't know what to do with myself. Two years and several jobs later I'd had enough, and decided to study Criminology and Social Policy at Loughborough. I had a great time – loved my new environment and my new mates, everything was going great. It was then that I got the call. I don't know how my aunt managed to tell me. My parents and sister had been killed in a plane crash.

I don't remember much, to be honest; the next year was a complete blur. All I do remember was the first night I didn't have a dream or nightmare that involved them. It was tough. Everybody wanted a piece of the story. My remaining sister and I were hounded, and police investigations put back the date of the funeral. Yet life around me carried on. People continued to smile, they had no idea my world had fallen apart. I was hurting more than I thought I was capable of managing – when I look back now I realise I wasn't. There were certainly times when I thought I couldn't cope, when I wanted the pain to go away. It never has and now I know it never will.

I used what happened to me as a driver. I became focused and threw myself into everything going so that I had as little thinking time as possible. I started working out in the gym and running a lot. I wanted my body to reflect the emotional pain, it helped against the emptiness. I graduated with a 2:1, taking on more roles of responsibility along the way. It was all part of the journey that led me to become Athletic Union President at Loughborough. I remember the results night. Four thousand people turned out to vote, the crowds were packed, and when it was read out I was ecstatic. Until the guilt hit me. It was then I realised that every new moment in my life to celebrate was going to come with a bittersweet edge.

I got selected to lead a charity project to Zambia, which helped put things into perspective. We delivered sports to children

who had nothing, but they were still smiling. There I was, upset about everything that had been taken away from me, while these children had nothing to start with. That was a big turning point for me. I decided to stop feeling sorry for myself, and with the help of those around me, I stopped being angry.

Until this point I thought I was untouchable. I had learned to shut myself away from those I loved, convinced myself that nothing mattered. But I hadn't dealt with it as well as I thought. I had been raised to be a gentleman by my mother and father, yet since the accident I always put myself first. I didn't like who I had become, that was a hard thing to admit. I sought the support of a psychologist and a mentor – little did I know how significant their influence would be and remain today.

When you are tested in life, your reaction can change you. Through my grief I lost touch with my values. I had forgotten who I was. I convinced myself and others that I was coping. It was my mentors who taught me not just to look at who I was, but who I wanted to be. I had to recreate myself and my behaviour. I then began to slowly mould myself back into the boy my parents had raised, and now into the man that I have become.

More bittersweet moments came and went. I set up a Volunteer Academy at Loughborough with just 20 volunteers. Two years later, we were supporting Team GB in their preparation camp at the university with over 600. Seven years after arriving at Loughborough it had become my safe haven, and leaving was a momentous occasion. I had already cut my ties with my hometown, this was it. I was out on my own, away from the protection of what I knew.

To me, being a man is to be able to be who you want to be and have the strength and conviction to go against expectations. I don't judge manhood by how many pints you drink, how much money you earn, or how many women you sleep with. In fact I think the opposite. Material possessions can come and go. When my time is up, I want to be remembered for the impact I made on others, not by how many cars I own in the garage, or how much money I have in the bank.

People will never know my own journey by looking at me, just as I will never know theirs. The important things in life aren't measurable, so it's hard to quantify how well I am living. A true reflection from those closest to me is all the validation I need. I'm better today than I was yesterday, and tomorrow I'll be better than today. I would change it all in a heartbeat, but that's not an option. Instead, I live my life, trying to be the best I can be.

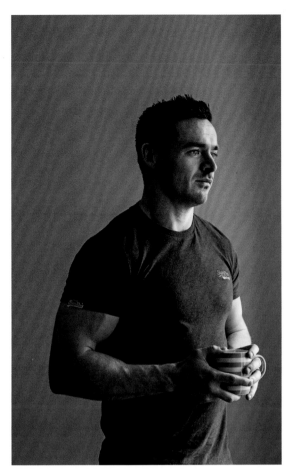

12 A BUMP IN THE ROAD

Anon

I have been putting this off for weeks. If I write about it, that means I have to think about it, remember it, relive it. I wasn't on the front line of a war, but my wife and I have had to undergo three rounds of IVF, which didn't seem far off at the time. Even now, writing this on a train with my wife 24 weeks pregnant, it feels too close for comfort.

Let's start with a slight amendment to the famous line by Ray Liotta in Goodfellas, 'As far back as I can remember I always wanted to be a father'. Actually, that wasn't me. Becoming a father wasn't something that I had ever given a great deal of thought to, it was just something I assumed would happen at some stage. How wrong I was.

We started trying as soon as we were married. Several months passed and my wife began to worry – she was convinced there was something wrong. But I didn't think too much of it, after all these things take time, don't they? Eventually she demanded that we seek medical advice, and after months of waiting we attended our first appointment at the fertility clinic. The consultant, having reviewed the results of various tests we had done in the preceding weeks, calmly asked if we had considered using a donor. My wife immediately broke down, and so the tone was set for the next couple of years.

Being faced with the prospect of not being able to have children hit us both hard, and it came to dominate our lives. It impacted my wife more than me to begin with, and this was the hardest part – seeing the woman I love retreat into herself and unravel in front of me. She didn't want to see anyone, she was convinced the world was against her. She was in a very dark place.

When we started to discuss the other options open to us, she began to come out of the darkness. But then it enveloped me. Initially I hadn't allowed myself to think about what being a father meant to me, what I would be missing out on if I couldn't be one. Once I did start to contemplate these possibilities I simply couldn't cope. I left my job. I couldn't think about what to do next. How could I when I couldn't see the point in any future without a family?

The IVF process is an emotional rollercoaster, to say the least. The excitement at the prospect of your life changing forever; the tough days of dealing with multiple injections; the stress of seeing my wife being wheeled into the operating theatre; the hope that the egg will fertilise; the joy when it does; the praying over the next few days that the cells will continue to grow and divide; the sense of anticipation when the embryo is transferred; the heart-wrenching moment the pregnancy test is negative; the ecstasy when the pregnancy test is positive.

We ended up going through three rounds of IVF and, at the point of breaking, we were successful on the last attempt. The experience over the last couple of years has certainly changed me and my relationship with others. I drifted away from friends along the way as I struggled to resonate with their issues and they with mine, but I now know where my priorities lie. What could have broken us as a couple has made my wife and me closer than ever. I am immensely proud of her for getting through it all, and proud of myself for the support I gave her. She helped me in return, but I like to think I'm still in credit. I hope so anyway, as I'm going to need all my wife's support when the time comes to welcome the little girl into the world we never thought we'd have.

13
ECHOES OF MY FATHER

Anon

Hands. That would take mine in his when I couldn't keep up with him.

His fingers, the shape of his nails, those knuckles where the flesh was red at the base of the index finger. My hand an echo of his, his etched in mine.

They would wave me off from the train platform, greet me with a curt salute when I made my return journey home. I can remember their every detail, the ridges in his nails, the short, jagged trace where he had bitten them.

How he would stroke my ear as a boy when I sat on his knee and hugged into him while he made a call on the old cord phone in the hallway.

I can't remember now if they were open or closed. They were warm, or rather they weren't cold.

His mouth. The scar to the right where a wasp had stung him and left a little red blemish after he had tried to set fire to its nest. A voice that I would have to interpret for my friends. His way of speaking, often with a raised finger over his lips – in concentration, in earnestness, in security? So that only the right words were uttered or heard? That voice, reassuring. The tongue that had been made thick with whisky over the years, always so clear and easy to me. The missing capped tooth; we had all laughed when it had fallen out. An empty darkness. Silent now. Mouth open, lips parted.

Eyes.
Grey, soft.
Smiling eyes. Always welcoming, even if they didn't like what they saw.
They would crease into a thin, infectious line when he was laughing. Not necessarily at anything we were laughing at, more likely a memory in his own head.
Cloudy now.

Frozen in that horrible moment.

He wasn't alone when it happened. He was in his own clothes and in his own home. Not in some faceless, cold ward where he was just another old man. That dignity could not be taken from him. He never got old, though age and illness had tried its damnedest.

This image of man, my template of man and everything a man should be. Desperately piecing him back together with the little details. Trying to keep a bit of him.

Gone.

Forever.

Just for five minutes more. To say? Nothing.
Just to hold his hand and listen to whatever he wanted to talk to me about. Restaurants-cars-antiques-roads-friends-universities – anything. To face what he was about to face. Together.

The perfect gentleman. Who had taken everything with such good grace. With dignity. Strength. Protecting us. He knew. He can't not have known. But he never said.

The world kept turning that day, even though the bottom had fallen out of mine. Nobody stopped. There were no grand gestures, no stopping of clocks. But he wouldn't have wanted that.
He would have wanted excellence.
He inspired it and celebrated it in others. Not to settle. Not to make do.
To aspire and to achieve.

To honour him is to be the best that I can be. To strive, to love. To put my loved ones first as he did.

I still have my moments of feeling hopelessly lost. Of indulgence. Of noise.
But these impressions of him, these glimpses of a great man remind me of where I have come from and everything I should be.

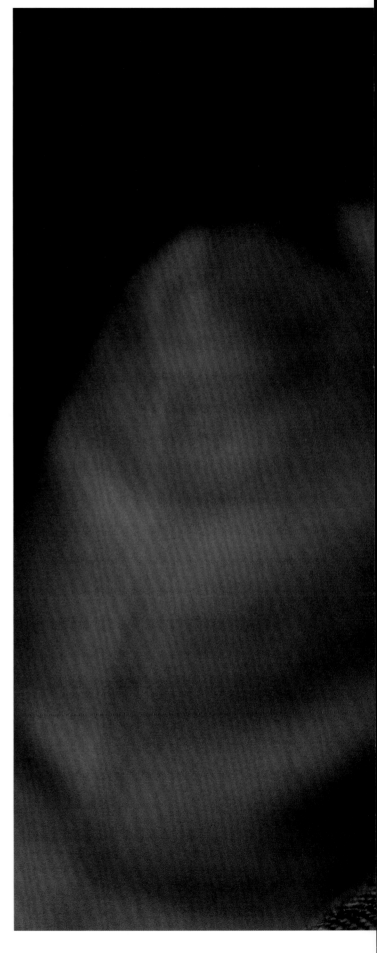

14 ROLE REVERSAL
Adam Sibley

I always used to think that the test of manhood was how physically strong you were, how you could handle yourself in a fight, and how many beers you could down on a Saturday night. It took a family member in need for me to understand its true meaning.

When I was 28 my mum was diagnosed with early onset dementia. Just as my adult life was in full swing I had to make a choice: did I continue to pursue my own dreams and ambitions, or did I put my mum first? I chose the latter.

I chose to sacrifice time with my friends, my hobbies, travelling, a career. But I knew it was the right decision and I didn't regret it. The ability to put someone else's needs in front of your own is the strongest test of character.

As a family we knew that my mum's prognosis wasn't good, and the likelihood was that things would get progressively harder. This didn't mean we just gave up. It taught me to not take any day for granted, and to make the best of every moment we had. I never focused on life getting worse. My mum would have done anything for me, so now it was my time to do something for her.

One of the biggest tasks in life is to learn how to control what you can, and not to worry about what you can't. Reacting positively to a bad situation will encourage others around you to not give up. If you want to change the atmosphere around you, you can. You may feel helpless, but more people are watching and feeding off your actions than you think.

Stopping to care for someone is the hard choice, not the easy choice. To me, manhood is about remaining strong and upbeat even in the most devastating of situations, not walking on by. No one should be judged by their circumstances, but rather how they handle themselves in them.

15 ALL GOOD IN THE FATHERHOOD

Darren

The soap shot out of the dispenser and landed in my little girl's hair, not in her hands as intended. As I tried to wash it out, the soap lathered up and bystanders could have been forgiven for thinking I was trying to wash her hair in the men's public toilet. Meanwhile, my boy was getting restless in his pushchair. We still had the automatic turnstile to negotiate on the way out, which had practically chewed us up and spat us out trying to get into the toilet in the first place. With my two toddlers in tow, by rights I should have known about the dedicated family toilet I could use instead, but while I might look like any other daddy of two small children on the surface, my little family is not what it seems. I am new to fatherhood.

Growing up, I'd taken it for granted that one day I'd be a family man with children of my own but, when the time came, it just didn't happen for me and my wife. After a good deal of soul-searching we embarked on the adoption process. After all, lots of modern families are blended, and by adopting we'd still get to experience the ups and downs of parenthood alongside our peers.

And so began a normal family life, with a twist. Sometimes we get along and sometimes we don't. We laugh, we cry, we annoy each other, we make mistakes and we learn from each other. We will do our best to help our children come to terms with their difficult start in life, but also encourage them to grab all of the opportunities it has to offer them as they grow up.

People tell us we've done an amazing thing for the children, but more so it's an amazing thing they've done for us.

16 SUPERDAD
Thomas Lynch

If I stop to think about movies that influenced my impression of fathers as I was growing up, the first two that come to mind are *Star Wars – The Empire Strikes Back* and *Superman*. The reveal of Darth Vader had a huge impact on me. What could drive a man to fight his own son? As for Superman, I wondered why his parents sent him so far from home on his own. It felt like these fathers were compelled to push their sons away. I wondered if perhaps that's what you had to do to allow your son to become a man.

As a kid, I knew what my dad did each day for work – I knew he built buildings and bridges. I knew he was no Superman, but I looked up to him and knew he worked hard. I could see it on his face, his hard-skinned hands, the dirt on his clothes, and from the way he fell asleep quickly in his seat at the end of the day.

When my wife told me she was pregnant, one of the first things that came to mind was a desire for my son to really know who I was. I also wondered what he would think of me, how he would relate to me, and whether he would know I worked hard. Between you and me, I wanted to be his Superman.

Holding my son for the first time humbled me. Though I knew he wasn't going to talk back, I wanted him to hear my voice telling him how much I loved him. I didn't know much about what being a dad meant, so I decided to start by giving him as much love as possible. The quiet five or ten minutes spent playing, reading or sitting on a bus with my son are the most precious moments. It's in those times that I get a little insight into his world.

My son is now seven, and the older he gets the more confident I feel about being dad. Like most, I'm making it up as I go along, doing what feels right and true. There's a little part of me that still strives to be his Superman, but the bigger voice in my head says I'm good enough for him. And that's good enough for me.

04

Carpe Diem

17 CHAIN REACTION

Frank Yeung

When I studied physics at university, I didn't particularly like it and my options seemed limited. I could either go into teaching as a professor, which I'd be terrible at; or leave and get a job, which I did. On graduation, I ended up working 90-hour weeks at Goldman Sachs as an Equities Sales Trader, which is fine if you love it, but I didn't.

But it wasn't a wasted experience. My job took me to New York on business quite a lot, and burritos are just huge over there. I went on trips to the city as much as I possibly could to glean inside information from the leading chain, hoping to make it translate back here in the UK. Then it was about making it all happen.

I opened the first branch of Poncho 8 in Spitalfields, which went swimmingly well from the offset – loads of work but a great little business. The second one went even better than the first, so a third seemed inevitable. However, on opening in Soho we lost everything we'd made over the previous two years in the space of four months. Though I'm glad of the experience, I would never, ever want to go through that again. It was the wrong product offering for the area, run from an over-rented property on a street without the requisite footfall. It looked busy but actually it wasn't – just the same people recirculating. It wasn't a cool restaurant, despite being in a cool area. It was a higgledy-piggledy site, so you had a kitchen downstairs, a poorly laid out operation on the ground floor, and then you had to walk upstairs. It seemed doomed to fail.

So as the shop haemorrhaged cash we opted to limit the damage and get rid of it. With the small premium we got for selling the lease, along with some more investment, we managed to open five more branches before deciding to finally leave. With each setback you learn something, but in business you tend to have to give away more and more equity to cover your losses. By the time we got to site number three, new investors had come on board who just cuckooed us out of the nest. Before I knew it, I

was still doing 80 hours a week, I wasn't enjoying it, and I was essentially working for someone else.

I had to get out of it, so my girlfriend and I set about starting something new. It was a kind of necessity. She was working in restaurants and waking up at crazy o'clock in the morning to do a job she didn't enjoy, and I wasn't enjoying what I was doing either. So together we made a leap, and opened Miss Tapas in Peckham. Now she loves her life. Miss Tapas is a year old now and is doing fantastically well. When we saw that there was another site going in Peckham, we were able to save up enough to launch Mr Bao, which has got off to a great start.

Just like when I was starting out with Poncho 8, I'm now serving and chatting with customers as well as overseeing the general running of things. The best bit about being your own boss is meeting such a variety of people. When I worked at Goldman Sachs, their recruitment processes were refined year on year so everyone was a carbon copy of each other. But now I meet people from all walks of life, whether they eat out with us, whether they're local or they've travelled to see us. Then there's the team. I work every day with people I would never have had the opportunity to meet. We've got artists who need a bit of extra money, foreigners and locals who want full-time employment, or those whose job is a welcome escape from something else in their lives. We nurture a little family – that's what happened with Miss Tapas, and that's what we're trying to do at Mr Bao.

When employing new staff, all I care about is that their default expression is a smile. You see these guys more than you see your own family, and it rubs off on the customers and the rest of the team. Anyone can learn how to fold a napkin, but you get far fewer problems if you've got personable staff. It's very difficult to be angry at someone who's cheerful. The system won't always run smoothly, so you need a team that knows they can do whatever they need to do to make the situation work. That comes with smiley people. They're the best investment.

18

AN OFFICER AND A GENTLEMAN

Ian James

I had no military history in the family. My closest relative to serve was a soldier who died at Gallipoli exactly a century ago, but somehow the army seemed like a good fit.

I had never really known what to do with myself after school. By the age of 22 I'd studied a bit and worked at various jobs, ranging from acting as a television extra to working as a door-to-door bacon salesman. But I had a very short attention span and became bored very rapidly. After a busy day I was left feeling empty, with no sense of achievement. I wanted to do something that mattered. Something that really, really challenged me.

The decision to become an officer came as an enormous surprise to my family and friends. On applying, I immediately ran into trouble. Although the military is much more balanced now than it was then, an obsession with social class can often lurk beneath the surface. One of the first steps in the process was a meeting with the Army Liaison Officer (ALO) responsible for my selection. Unfortunately he had other ideas. I was completely unprepared for our meeting, and spent an hour being humiliated for my cheap suit, my shoes, my tie, my school, my lack of military connections. Essentially for having the cheek to aspire to becoming an officer at all. He didn't want to hear about my fitness, my brains, my teamwork skills or how I behaved in a crisis. All he wanted to know was what the hell I was doing wasting his time.

I left his office angry and despondent, but despite this terrible start I could still put myself forward for officer selection. Although I was convinced he would undermine me at every opportunity, I could still go down to Westbury and sit the three days of mental and physical testing before the Army Commissioning Board. I made my mind up to give it a go, and booked a date.

It was then that my plans were turned upside down. I broke my collarbone while out running one icy winter morning –

so badly that the fractured end of the bone almost poked out through the skin. The rehabilitation was horrendous, but the worst part was having to wait for four months to see if it had healed sufficiently to attempt the selection board. I finally turned up for the start of my course carrying a bad injury and a stinking report from the ALO.

I was expecting to fail, but I concentrated on doing the absolute best I could on every challenge. At the back of my mind I kept thinking about how bored I was with my pedestrian life beforehand and repeating to myself all the criticism I had received. That gave me all the motivation I needed. I left the board not knowing how I'd got on, hoping I'd done enough to persuade them to accept me.

Eventually I heard back via a formal letter. I had been accepted at the officer training academy at Sandhurst, and was due to start in January. I was delighted. I started my officer training and never looked back.

I can't do justice to all the things I've experienced in the eight years since joining the army, but I'll include some highlights: I've completed the infamous Commando training programme and taken troops to war in Afghanistan (and brought them all back). I've skied in the Arctic Circle at midnight, in -35°C, and travelled all over the world. I've competed in sports for my regiment, and recently became a military SCUBA diving and skiing instructor. I'm currently training as a doctor and will go back to the army as a Medical Officer on completion. I even spend time working with young people aspiring to join the army, although I never mention their suits or shoes.

19
TOP GUNS
Jovin Harper

When I graduated from Loughborough University in 2008, my life was very much on track. I had been a successful young sportsman and attained a bachelor's degree in Civil Engineering. I had always aspired to be in the military, particularly as a pilot, and I applied later that year to join the Royal Navy. It was a long haul, but finally I began my training in April 2010 having passed the rigorous selection processes.

Unfortunately, my timing was not great. Halfway through my second term of officer training, the 2010 Defence Spending Review struck. Royal Navy flying training was ceased indefinitely. This left me in a strange situation. I remained employed, but with no specific role. I took short-term placements in various short-staffed departments around the navy. This dragged on, and the wait changed from months to years. The realisation dawned that I would not start my flying training any time soon, and I began to doubt if it was ever destined to happen. The lack of any career progression was so demoralising, I considered leaving to pursue other options many times.

In a lucky coincidence, my girlfriend and I stumbled across the opportunity to buy into a gym owned by a mutual friend in our local town. It was going bankrupt, but we knew we could sort it out. Bolstered by a recruitment job I retained with the navy, we set about turning the gym around. I wasn't flying, but I was able to throw my efforts into something else I had a passion for.

It turned out to be tougher going than we'd initially predicted. I wound up having to finish work in the afternoon only to head straight to the gym until the early hours, often going to bed covered in dust to grab only a few hours sleep before doing it all again the next day. My girlfriend was also working 90-hour weeks for just £350 per month, sometimes less. We started to despair, but eventually the hard work paid off and people were able to see the results of our labours. Membership increased steadily after the first year, and we keep building on this success.

At the end of 2013, I finally began my flying training and am now achieving my dream of becoming an operational Naval Aviator. There are still negatives – I am very old for my stage of training, and uncertainties in postings delayed our marriage plans – but they are outweighed by the positives.

Life very rarely goes perfectly to plan, but opportunities do come along to improve yourself or your situation. I came close to quitting many times, but if we had just given up I would not have a job that I enjoy as much as I do now. Sometimes it takes a lot of hard graft for no immediate reward before you realise your goal.

We couldn't bury my father until almost a month after he had passed away. Winter temperatures of -15°C meant the ground was too hard to dig. My route to work took me past the funeral parlour where dad lay waiting every day for four weeks. It was a long, draining month.

I was working as a project manager at a steel fabrication company. After leaving school to train as an apprentice welder, I'd worked my way up through the ranks from the workshops onto construction sites and then office staff. A proper career. However, two years later our company was hit by the recession and went into receivership. It was a family-run firm, one I very much felt part of, but it was over. Just like that.

With minimal redundancy money, no income, and a seemingly endless stream of dad's affairs to sort out, it was a tough summer. But that September my partner Michelle revealed I was going to become a dad. So I decided to open a music studio… Playing guitar in bands had always been a big part of my life. I'd met great people, made genuine friends and always dreamed of running a studio – I'd even looked into it before my career had taken over.

Starting a new business in the depths of a recession, while expecting a baby and after an intensely emotional period might not seem like a good idea, but with the job gone the time had come. We had countless 'what if?' conversations. What if the business fails? What if we can't pay the mortgage or buy nappies? But there was another, bigger question: what if we never tried? This was my chance and I had to take it. Before I knew it I was in a solicitor's office, signing papers and beginning my new life.

On the anniversary of dad's passing, a routine scan showed a major problem with our baby. There was a 99% chance he would not survive if the pregnancy managed to reach full term. After weeks of hospital visits, consultations, tears and long

20
DIGGING DEEP
Andy Gurski

hours of deliberation, we came to the agonising decision to terminate the pregnancy. The pain was unbearable. Our child was born asleep on the anniversary of dad's funeral.

I had to dig deep in the following weeks to motivate myself to get out of bed, never mind build a business from scratch. But after everything that had happened – losing my dad, my job, then my son – I was more determined than ever.

Each and every day was a challenge, both mentally and physically. I was in a bad place and it was affecting my personality massively. But my dad had taught me to work hard for what I wanted in life. Holding onto that thought got me through my darkest days.

With the help of family and friends, the coming weeks saw my business slowly take shape. Together with my brother Paul, a carpenter by trade, we pooled our backgrounds in construction to turn an empty shell of a building into a functioning music studio. With every task completed during the build I began to feel happier and better about myself, and getting out of bed no longer became a problem. By the end of May 2012 Aspect Studios was ready to open. It was a fantastic feeling. I'd come through a period of gut-wrenching lows over those two years, but I'd found the strength and determination to follow my dreams, to build a new future. And it's a strength I believe is in us all.

05

Big Boys Do Cry

21
BARBERSHOP BLUES
Ken Hermes

I'm what they call a survivor of suicide, which is a strange thing to call it.

Suicide. It's a horrible word. It sends shivers down your spine and brings up barriers in most people. It is the single biggest killer of under 45s in the UK. A staggering 80% of cases are men. Statistics show that somebody takes their life every 120 minutes in the UK. With this being such a huge issue, why do we feel that we can't speak about it and the mental health conditions that link to it?

I lost my dad to suicide when I was 15. There was no note, no warning. One day I woke up and he wasn't there anymore. It hit me really hard. My dad and I were best friends, we were so close. The night before he died we had a normal night. We were smoking and drinking, I was playing his favourite songs on my guitar, we talked about everything. It felt that night like he was really wearing his heart on his sleeve, but he didn't tell me how depressed he was feeling, I had no idea. I didn't even know my dad took antidepressants. I was only young, he was probably trying to protect me.

As time passed, I felt that I couldn't talk to anyone about what I was going through anymore, everyone had grown tired of hearing it. Kids at school blocked me out, there was clearly a big taboo around the subject. I don't think my dad had anyone to speak to in that respect either. Maybe it was a pride thing. His pride may have cost him his life.

I haven't felt able to speak out until now. Until the Lions Barber Collective came about. When I heard that barbers were raising awareness of suicide, I knew I had to get involved, but I had no way of knowing how big this project would become.

It started slow. I was asked to film a short video blog explaining my loss and why I – a non-barber – was getting in with a group of barbers. That video had 14,000 views in seven days. It proved to me that speaking out not only helped me, but could

help others that have lost, or are going through depression themselves. Together with founders Tom Chapman *(pictured)* and Pat Barry, we are developing training that has never been seen before.

The truth is that men will speak to their barbers about things they wouldn't tell anybody else. The #BarberTalk program teaches barbers how to recognise, talk, listen and advise their clients. With this comes the responsibility to remain confidential, provide a safe haven for clients, and offer help where necessary. Talking about suicide does not make it more likely to happen. By breaking the taboo, we could save a life.

Society is slowly accepting the conversation, so why not talk to your barber?

There are a few tricks you need to keep up your sleeve when you're drinking between half a litre and a litre of vodka a day. You have to know lots of good hiding places to stash bottles. Under the hedgerow of the front garden is not bad, so you can pick it up when you leave for work. You have to know lots of places you can duck into in private, where you can pour the vodka from the big glass bottle into plastic water bottles, setting you up for the day. Train station toilets are good for this. You get to know all the codes for the security doors. You have to be good at covering up the signs. Antibiotic hand gel masks the smell. Wearing contact lenses gives you an excuse for bleary eyes.

It's an exhausting, full-time job. You have to know where you're going to be and when, so you can plan how you're going to buy enough booze to get you through the next stretch. God forbid you ever get caught out with nothing left after the shops have closed. Holidays and family visits are tough, especially if they're in the countryside. It's hard to explain why you have to go four miles to the off-licence in the village at half past nine on a Tuesday evening, when the true answer is that your hands are getting shaky and you need a 70cl bottle of 37.5% Glen's vodka for £11.99 to see you through the night.

Contrary to popular belief, being an alcoholic takes a great deal of discipline and organisation. You have to remember what the hell you said to people the night before and where you've stashed the bottles. You have to keep track of when different shops are open until. You have to organise your money and budget carefully. You need pre-prepared excuses for all sorts of contingencies. You have to keep deodorant handy, and know where to duck out of sight for a discreet top-up ('just going up this alley and behind that skip, darling, back in two'). In short, you have to spend an enormous amount of time lying through your teeth.

Inevitably, you fail. You get caught out more and more often – people catching a whiff of your breath, housemates finding

22 DRINKING GAMES
Anon

bottles behind cupboards, forgetting entire conversations you had the previous evening. Sooner or later, you lose control.

By the time I was ready to admit the problem and ask for help, I couldn't go more than four hours without alcohol before I would start feeling serious withdrawal symptoms. I couldn't sleep the night through without getting up to drink. They say you have to hit rock bottom before you can get sober, but it's different for everyone. All it really means is that a previously tolerable set of circumstances has become intolerable. I didn't crash a car, get fired, hurt anyone or get arrested. My girlfriend didn't leave me (although she was pretty fed up). I just realised that I couldn't bear to go on like this, not even for one more day.

How did I end up at this point? I don't really know. Understanding root causes is one of the central tenets of modern psychology, but it can only take you so far. If a cigarette butt has started a fire in your house, stubbing it out won't stop the house burning down. There's a genetic component in alcoholism, but genetics are misunderstood and oversimplified. There's no alcoholism gene. Hereditary factors can make you more susceptible, but there are no certainties. Environmental factors play a part. My mum died when I was nine and my dad drank heavily, but a lot of people go through a lot worse and never have a problem. In my case, I simply drank more and more, and it was never enough.

I tried to stop by myself, which I now know was ridiculous. When you're dependent on a substance, stopping with no medical support is very dangerous. You can collapse and have a seizure, or blackout and wake up in A&E or a police station (or dead). Twelve hours after I stopped, I was in so much pain I could barely stand. I phoned my GP, dropping the phone

several times, who advised me to have a drink immediately. When I was referred to a Drug and Alcohol Recovery Team, they got me to cut down my drinking over a period of a month. I then moved on to a 'community detox', where I stopped drinking altogether and stayed at home for a week taking a drug called Librium – a relaxant which stops you feeling those withdrawal symptoms while the alcohol works its way out of your system. After a week I was entirely sober.

So here's the thing. It was easy for me to stop. But I was lucky. One of the reasons people find it so hard is that they've already lost so much – marriage, children, job, shelter – and there doesn't seem to be any point making an effort. But none of these problems are unsolvable, no matter what you think. The worst thing you can imagine happening usually turns out to be not that bad when you get there.

A lot of men – men in particular – find it almost ludicrously hard to ask for help. Old jokes about not asking for directions aside, by and large we don't like to admit vulnerability. Being an alcoholic means being a loser, a weak-willed, helpless tramp.

The thing is, I'm proud of being a recovering alcoholic. I think it's one of my best qualities. Yeah, I'm an alcy. I don't drink. I have a disease where if I do drink, I get addicted. You wouldn't call a cancer survivor a loser, would you? I'm a recovering alcy; that makes me hard as fuck.

It's been almost two years since I stopped drinking. It's easy. OK, maybe it's not so easy, but it's a lot easier if you ask for help. Children sometimes try to deal with problems by themselves because they're embarrassed and they don't know better. That's understandable, they're children. Men ask for help.

23 HONEST TOIL
Abizer Kapadia

Every story seems to be about happiness. Self-help guides abound. What are you selling with your condensed answers expounding the secrets to success? That sentence is a contradiction. To expound: 'to give a detailed statement of, set forth'. To condense: 'To make more concise; abridge or shorten'. Whatever it is, it has only ever brought me unhappiness.

I contradicted myself daily. Like an actor cast as a jovial gentleman. Outwardly I was forever happy, calm, and easy. Inwardly I suffered an endless sadness.

My story begins as a teenager. What I long for now was once normal for me. I bumbled through life, lazy and unaware. I couldn't understand how anyone could be sad. Life was too good. I was too happy.

It came out of nowhere. Slowly crept up on me. Imperceptible until too late. I withdrew from the world around me. Bit by bit rejected what kept me sane. Quit my job. Moved in with my parents. Locked myself in my room. Stopped calling people. Stopped answering the phone. If a social situation was unavoidable I would attend wearing my mask of happiness. Drink heavily. Disappear silently.

Months went by. No one noticed. Not even my parents. I stopped shaving. Showered only when the smell began to sicken me. My anxiety spread to sound. I'd wake in the morning and listen. Listen to make sure no one was in the bathroom, or on the landing, or near the stairs. Making sure the coast was clear. Only then making a rapid dart to the toilet to release 11 hours worth of liquid pressing hard on my bladder. 11 hours. I was sleeping longer. Not sleeping; lying in my bed researching.

I'd become a diligent scientist. In four years of university, studying chemistry and then more chemistry, I can only claim to have worked one of those years. But now here I was in my lab. Studying hard. What's the most painless way to die? How

can I take my own life without harming anyone else? How much is a one-way ticket to Beachy Head?

The Samaritans saved me countless times, though I never called the number. Never heard their voice. Try searching suicide. Their number will turn up. It made me think of how hard life is for my mother already, and how much harder it would get if I were to leave. My father, he's strong, but he's done too much for me to desert him now.

My saviour was unexpected. It was my brother who discovered my despair. He noticed it in my absence. We never got on. Not once until the age of 21. But he was there, when it came to it. He was there when I needed him most.

He'd seen it before. Perhaps in himself, but certainly in his patients. A psychiatrist by trade. The success of the family. It started slowly, the recovery. Peppered with dips, relapses big and small, on the journey to somewhat normal.

The first steps back out in the real world were far from easy. I didn't have anyone to call. Ten days of yoga for £10. It will get me out of the house. I attended purposefully and industriously. It gave me a glimpse of peace. But it wasn't enough. I was still withdrawn – spoke softly, avoiding eye contact – but at least I was speaking.

On returning from an evening yoga session, I would sit downstairs and eat my dinner in front of the TV. For me it was progress. It had been many months since I'd last remained in a public space for more than a few minutes. A space where someone could wander by. It had also been a similar amount of time since I had last eaten a proper meal. Not snatched bites when I was sure no one was around. For the next eight months I attended a class almost every day.

I can't tell you what helped me get through it. Perhaps it was time. Maybe I was never depressed at all. Just endlessly sad. But for two years there was no escape. And now I felt, on occasion, the warmth of happiness. For two years after that I did all I could to make myself better. Forced myself out into the world. Attended a silent meditation retreat. Rekindled great friendships that, at the heart of it, were never lost. For a while it all felt better. For a while.

It crept up on me again, in earnest, not too long ago. I'd had minor setbacks before, but this time was different. It was darker. A realisation that on my journey to recovery I'd got one thing wrong. What I do, or the way I do it, was dragging me back into the void.

I know now that my battle with the sadness is ongoing. I can't get complacent when it starts to feel OK. But I know what to do for me. I've started working on it. This is my new life – toiling away in the fields of happiness. Happiness takes work. Hard, laborious, backbreaking work.

I never had been good at reading the right signs. After ignoring my doctor's diagnosis of acute depression, I had ended a promising relationship, quit my corporate job, and booked a one-way flight to Australia.

Several months on I was hitching a ride in a beaten-up, second-hand campervan with some bohemian hippies down the famous East Coast. By this point I had endured frequent demoralising mishaps caused by the rash and irrational decision-making endemic to my condition. I had already lost my passport and pretty much all of my money. I'd hoped that travelling and living free would serve as a distraction to my problems, but these misfortunes fed my depression, which in turn had started to erode away the best of my character.

One traveller of the convoy really stands out in my memory. Max was a Frenchman who typified the look and character of the group, with thick dreadlocks, piercing blue eyes and a collection of tribal tattoos on sun-bronzed skin. He was earning his way around the continent by busking outside shopping centres and picking up farm work.

It pained me with jealousy to see that he had made his travelling experience work for him. At one point, not long before we parted company, I asked for his advice.

"I just don't know what it is I'm supposed to do," I said.

"Nobody really knows, bro, and I can't tell you. But that's why it's so important to follow the signs."

This added to my frustration. I felt when travelling I could never get any real answers. I tried my best to go along with the flow as a free spirit, yet I was always trying to hold onto the professional pragmatist that I left behind in my corporate, city existence.

24 SIGNS *Matthew Kynaston*

"I don't know what the signs are, I've never seen them." I desperately pushed out every word as if the extra emphasis would convince him to divulge a real solution to my problems.

"Maybe you're choosing not to see them," he said.

He was right.

My mind backtracked to the last days and moments with the woman who once loved me. The battle in my head between the voices that told me to stay with her, and those that urged me to go. I remember turning off a radio station that was playing love songs; the aching in my stomach and the tears that welled in my eyes were weaknesses that had held me back before.

Instead, I listened to the signs I was supposed to listen to as a man. The anger and disappointment that would spur me on for the next year. The envy that used to enrage me, especially when I locked into my Facebook news feed; scrolling through reels of pictures and videos of peers who documented their worldly travels, each new exotic discovery marked with a selfie.

It was my turn. I booked my flight, and let her go.

But I didn't. We sent one another message upon message. I couldn't go for a whole day without knowing what she was doing, and hearing that she missed me. I needed that. With every 'like' on my status updates of beautiful sunset shots, I also needed her approval.

For four months we went back and forth battling for each other's attention. We tried moving on, but then also tried making it work. I pushed her away, then yearned for her attention. I embraced my freedom when I felt it was mine to have, and tried to fuck away her hold over me. But no matter how many women I woke up next to, I couldn't let her go.

Not even when she told me to leave her alone. With 21,000 messages and 10,500 miles between us, and after countless arduous cycles of tearful and angry arguments, she blocked me on Facebook.

Where I had lost all contact with her, I had also lost my control over her. She was free. In the months to come, she became my obsession as my self-loathing seethed and swelled. Within a couple of weeks of that road trip, things went from bad to worse. I just wasn't able to comprehend all of my losses, given where I had come from and the reasons for my escape. I had failed, and without the mental strength to pick myself up – nor the support network to do it for me – I began to plan my suicide.

An advert for a suicide prevention hotline saved my life, a sign in its most literal sense. I spent the next week in a psychiatric ward.

My road to recovery was long and beautiful. I began to understand that the signs that appeared to appease my jealousies and dissatisfactions were misleading. By drowning in sadness and self-loathing I could no longer see that I had become obsessive, abusive and controlling. I learned instead that it was better to choose my life's direction on a set of criteria based on becoming a kinder and happier person.

We're all on a path. When you adopt the right kind of thinking it can make the signs seem a lot easier to interpret, particularly if you choose one of purpose and happiness.

Solo travel can be one of the most rewarding experiences in any lifetime. But travelling alone with an unchecked mental illness can prove deadly. I am writing my memoirs in tribute to those who shared the weight of my burdens and helped me stop running, to find my way home.

I've had ten years now of not being quite sure how my brain works. I woke up when I was 22 years old to feel the last year of misery hit me all at once – a conclusive punch in the face of proper sadness. My experience of depression has gone from complete naivety and unconscious buckling, to admiring its power and working with it to come to a happy medium.

I had finished uni, had pissed around travelling for a year, and was a fun, optimistic person. I was cocky, I made out like I didn't give a crap. Nothing fazed me really. But the real me underneath that macho bravado was a nice lad who'd got lost in adulthood. Don't get me wrong, that's the same story for most kids. Life's a piss-take and then you're on your own. Things start not going as well as they usually do, you get a bit sad.

But this wasn't just a bit sad. It was like an internal vacuum cleaner sucking my soul away, drawing my face in, bagging up my personality. I got aggressive, drank more, did drugs, tried to fight it off in all the wrong ways. The problem was I didn't know how to equip myself with the right tools to slay it. We weren't told in school that there is a one in four chance that you will suffer from a mental health problem. Or that we might one day have an illness that could whisper suicidal thoughts to us. If I could have known at the time, I wouldn't have fought, drank, done drugs. I would have told my family, my friends, my doctor.

But it wasn't just my lack of knowledge about the illness that was stopping me from speaking up. It was the thought that everyone would think I was a wimp, that I'd have to carry the burden of the stigma unaided. Let's face it, when you're in your twenties you have complete freedom to do what the hell you like. The number one thing that most of us want to do is have fun. Opening up about depression to a group of 20 year olds felt like excluding myself permanently from a decade of fun, so I just didn't. Fun was the only refuge from the pitch-black darkness in my head when I was alone.

25 CURTAIN CALL
Tim Grayburn

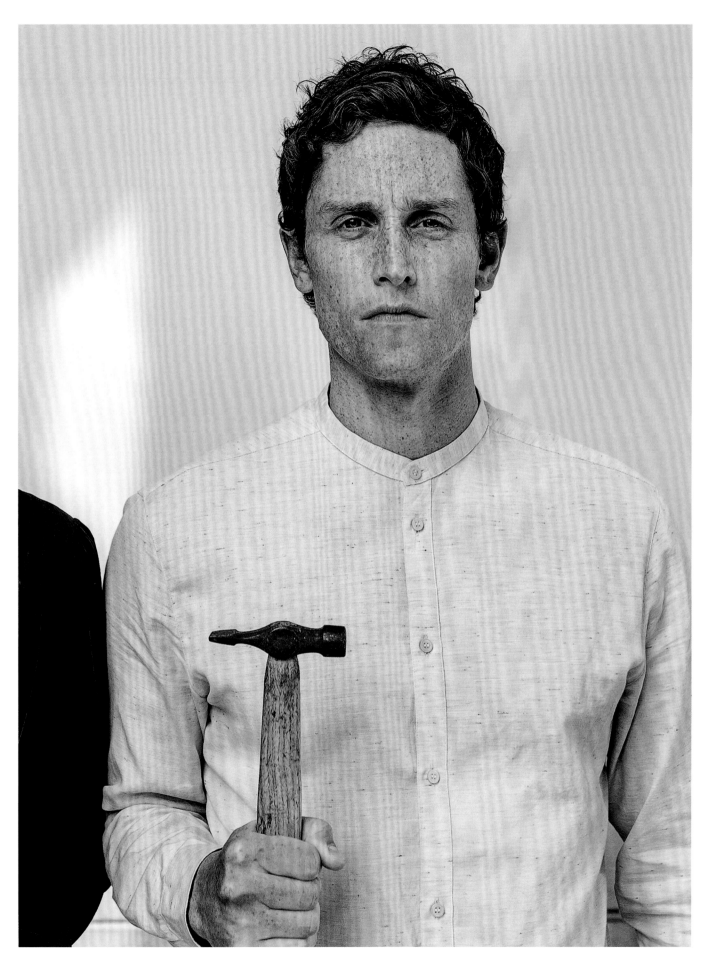

That was the exact opposite of what I should have done. I wish I'd dealt with it head on and tried to get myself better before I let it take up permanent residence in my brain. The depression was hanging pictures on the wall of my skull, when it could have been a temporary visitor.

In 2015-16 my partner and I toured with a theatre show about my experience with depression, and how we as blokes need to talk about our problems before it's too late. 78% of suicides are by men, and this proportion has been the same for over a decade. It's pretty obvious that not enough men are allowing themselves to talk about it, going undiagnosed and untreated. To those who don't believe in depression, I would ask, what healthy-minded person would take their own life just to relieve mental pain? It's a very real illness, it hurts more than any physical pain I've ever had.

The show has helped me so much. It's been tough to be on stage talking about my own issues, but it's been a therapeutic and rewarding ride. And the stats are on my side – 40 depressed people out of 100 could take on the other 60 easily. The feedback has been incredible and it feels good. It helps a lot to know that the show is making people speak up and be proud. There's no one pretending to be depressed, you could spot it a mile off if there was. We've had stories from people all over Australia and the UK. We're all in it together, and fingers crossed the stigma will disappear alongside our fear of speaking the truth.

06

For the Love of Life

I grew up in Kennington, South East London, where there was a great community feel. Everybody knew everybody; every family knew everybody else's family. I spent most of my time trying to stay out of trouble by riding my bike at Brixton skate park with my friends. We'd spend all our days there, riding, jumping, hanging out – that was the place to be.

When I was about 14 I started to take BMX riding more seriously. I worked at an indoor facility teaching kids how to drive Go Karts, and used the money I earned to go to more professional races and hang out with champion riders. I would train with them to find out exactly what they were doing to make themselves so elite. I missed out on the Olympics, so aged 19 I decided to become a DJ instead.

My brother is a big reggae DJ and I started going to the clubs with him to learn the craft, applying the same discipline and focus that BMX had taught me. My brother worked on a radio station called Choice FM and I managed to get a spot on there too. No one was playing grime music at that time, so we were able to bring in all the new artists. That's where we found acts like Ms Dynamite and So Solid Crew. We opened our own recording studio over in Walthamstow and discovered Dizzee Rascal, Wiley and Lethal Bizzle.

Unfortunately the station got sold, so I decided to return to BMX and put my energy back into something that I owned. I had enjoyed working with the youngsters on the radio, so when I got a phone call asking me to give some kids BMX lessons, it was an easy decision to make.

I met up with the kids at Brockwell Park in Brixton every week and it slowly grew. I took the kids down to a disused BMX track, moved a lot of the rubbish that was there, made a circuit, and organised a fun day. After that, the council asked if I could do it every week. I agreed, but only if they spent some money on the track to get it revamped. We raised about £17,000 and Peckham BMX Club was born.

26 HALF PIPE DREAMS

CK Flash

The kids started winning all the big races in the UK. In 2008, we won the National and British titles, and a year later the European title. In 2012 we built a brand new track at Burgess Park, and soon after we saw one of our boys get World Number Three while our girls got World Number Two and Three. So the story goes on. We keep improving each year, and my aim is to build more BMX tracks across the country. In the meantime, my main focus is getting funding to expand the club. We want to buy a building and install a music studio, radio station and a gym where the kids can train and have somewhere to chill out.

First and foremost, Peckham BMX Club has a constitution of good behaviour. It's all about your attitude and how you portray yourself out in the world. We teach life skills like healthy eating and drinking, the importance of getting enough sleep, and punctuality. If you're late for the track, you're going to be late for school, college and work. We teach the young people to be organised and focused on what they're doing, and if they don't do it we discipline them. If they're misbehaving at school or home, they'll be washing all 40 bikes and won't be riding the track until they've learned their lesson. It's important to teach them this because many of our riders go on to take part in the Olympic programme in Manchester. If their behaviour isn't up to scratch there, they'll simply be thrown out.

I know what these kids are capable of, and if they put into practice everything I've taught them I'm confident that they can become champions. When you put in that kind of hard work and focus, it's a great relief to see them actually winning at what they do.

I have won the Volunteer of the Year awards with British Cycling, we won the Achievement Through Sport Award at the Spirit of London Awards, and the icing on the cake was being awarded an MBE in February 2016 for my contribution to youth sport in BMX. But the best thing for me is to know that I've created something from nothing – taken a disused, neglected track to build one of the largest in the UK. I have set a foundation with the people that come here to carry on my legacy when I'm gone. This way we've got a conveyor belt for happy, healthy youths to enter the world.

27 BOTH SIDES OF THE LENS

Harry Macqueen

In seven years as a professional actor, I'd never been on this side of the camera before. Things came to a head when I inherited some money in a will. I had always intended to make my own film at some point, just not necessarily this early in my career. But I wanted to do something with the money that would have made the person who left it to me proud. That's how it all started.

Having worked a decent amount in film and television, I knew something of how to go about making a film, and how not to go about it too. It's important in life to take risks and get out of your comfort zone, not to worry about failing. It's tremendously freeing to know that you'll learn even by fucking up.

I'm interested in the unsaid, and cinema is a medium custom-built to examine that. I wrote the screenplay over Christmas 2012 and we shot it in 13 days the following February. I knew that I wanted to make a film in which the literal journey would mirror the emotional one. More broadly speaking, I wanted to explore the blurred line between friendship and love.

Starting with that idea in mind, the characters grew from there. But I was learning everything from scratch. I still had no idea how to produce a film, nor how we were going to cast it. One of the biggest challenges was finding someone to play the lead – a musician who was very viscerally defined in my mind.

Lori was perfect for the part in pretty much every way, but the project had to accommodate her own gigging schedule. My intention from the outset was that I shouldn't be in the film myself, but once I'd persuaded Lori to get on board, we just didn't have the money or space in the car for anyone else, so I stepped in.

There were just six of us that made the film – cast and crew, some folks I knew, and some suggested by friends. We all went down to Cornwall and treated it like the road trip that it was

– just a lovely, intimate collaboration between a small band of like-minded people. The organic nature of the way we worked comes across on screen. It was fun in a two-hours-sleep-in-two-weeks-and-a-year-of-constant-anxiety kind of way…

I wanted to make a film that meant something to my contemporaries and me, because I was in that period of life when not everything really makes that much sense yet. I wanted to make a film that spoke to my generation about the no man's land between leaving education and whatever comes next. I wanted to make a truthful story about human interaction, quietly and honestly observing two people at this junction in their lives within the context of contemporary Britain.

We managed to make *Hinterland* Britain's first carbon-neutral feature film, forgoing a DVD run and releasing it on Video on Demand channels on the day of its UK cinema premiere. It was no mean feat on the budget we had. The film has now played everywhere from London to China, appearing at many prestigious film festivals and winning awards along the way. It was nominated Best Feature at Raindance in 2014 and Best Debut Film at Beijing Film Festival in 2015, with a few more on the horizon. We were even long-listed for a BAFTA. I wanted to make a film that resonated with the people who watched it, and I'm very proud that it has.

I believe that everybody in life has a purpose, and I found that purpose one night at the age of ten, when I came across an old hip hop production CD while putting the rubbish out. I stuck it straight into my computer, and that was the moment my life changed forever. At first I was just making very simple music – mixing tracks together and experimenting with rap lyrics. By the age of 11, I could call myself a music producer.

For musicians in Iran to legally produce and perform music, they need to get official approval from the government. Only certain forms of music receive licenses, and politically-critical rap is not one of them.

I created an underground studio which I shared with about 40 other musicians. We rapped freely about philosophy, politics, the government and the problems people face in our country. I was the youngest by far, with a really fast flow and the ability to memorise about 50 verses of rap.

One night, in 2012, I was putting the finishing touches to my debut album, when the 'morality police' raided the studio. They seized my album, all of the equipment, and arrested everyone they found.

Luckily I was out of the studio at the time. My mum called and said it wasn't safe for me to stay. I needed to flee the country. She informed me that someone would call me and I needed to trust them. I soon got the call – the stranger told me to take a small bag with a few clothes. He picked me up in a car in the middle of the night and I soon fell asleep. Each time I opened my eyes I was in a different city. We drove through Turkey, Spain and France. I finally arrived in London as a political refugee.

Since then I've been making music, making connections with other rappers, and trying to recreate my album. I have ten different rappers from different countries singing on the album

28 MAKING TRACKS *TabraE*

in their native languages. I've performed at several festivals and club nights in London, where I've started to build a fanbase for myself.

Last year I completed the 'Amy's Yard' music programme set up by the Amy Winehouse Foundation. This amazing experience gave me the opportunity to work with the producer Urban Monk in the same studio where Amy created many of her tracks. The Foundation gave me a once-in-a-lifetime experience to continue my musical journey and accomplish my dreams.

29 VIVA CAPOEIRA!

Boneco de Sousa

As far back as I can remember, my father left for work early and only returned after we had gone to bed. We rarely saw him. My mother was, and still is, the queen of the house, a *Rainha da Casa*. She was always our role model and our inspiration to face life beyond the boundaries of our situation.

My family of three brothers and three sisters was born and raised in a favela (shanty town) in the city of Fortaleza, Brazil. From the age of ten or eleven, my older sisters looked after us while our mother went to work alongside my father. My two brothers and I had to start working at a similar age to contribute to the household income, helping out at the family business in the city centre.

One day, my older brother announced he had been to Capoeira. What? Capoeira? Nobody really paid attention to the word. My mother was angry. There was a curfew imposed by the military government at that time and she was worried for his safety. I saw her beating him without understanding what was happening. I was only seven at the time. The next day I saw him getting ready to sneak out again. I wanted to go too, but he refused to take me so I followed in secret. I was very scared. Being so young, going through areas that were unfamiliar, not even knowing where I was going or the way back home. I saw him disappear into a large building at the other side of a football pitch. As soon as I got inside I heard the music and saw a Capoeira class for the first time. Children were practising, dancing, jumping and playing musical instruments. I couldn't be still, so I began imitating my brother's movements in the corner of the room. The teacher saw me and asked, "Who is that boy there, who is he with?" My brother, furious at seeing me, acknowledged I was with him. He immediately invited me in, "Vamos treinar!" Let's get training!

That moment changed my life. I have kept Capoeira with me ever since. Four of my five siblings are also capoeiristas, and I feel at home with my family and music all around us. It has

impacted on me socially, professionally and personally in ways that I never anticipated. The things I have achieved in my life have been made possible by Capoeira.

Brazil wasn't good to us when we were growing up. For poor families living in the favelas, discrimination was normal – we had no choice but to accept the hierarchy and our position in society. Jobs, school places and healthcare were only accessible according to social class. My education didn't come from an inadequate school system, but from my parents and from Capoeira. My foundation as a person, as a man, came from them. I learned through witnessing positive attitudes, struggles, achievement, resistance and respect. I learned that Capoeira can give power to people, because it gave it to me.

My siblings came to Europe in the 1990s. When I joined my sisters in London to help develop a dance school, it was a huge culture shock, seeing people engulfed by their intense, work-focused routines. I felt homesick, miles away from Brazil, but I could see how the power of Capoeira remained in us, providing an internal equilibrium. I came to believe that I could share this with others. Last year we gathered as a group of friends to establish a community association whose main objective is to use Capoeira as a social tool to enhance wellbeing, cultural exchange and promote community involvement.

From my childhood in Brazil, Capoeira engaged me and helped me to develop into a man who can contribute to society. I hope to open the minds of children and young people, to help them learn to respect not only their own culture but those of others.

07

I Am

30 CROSS PURPOSES

Laurie Brown

I was 22 when my friend asked me to be in her final year piece for her degree in Contemporary Performance. Frustrated by showing work in arts venues that only reached a limited audience, she made a piece to be shown in public. *Walking:Holding* was an experiential performance that involved one audience member at a time walking through the city holding hands with a range of different people, one after the other, on a carefully designed route. I was to be one of the people the audience held hands with, but this time during these performances I would wear women's clothes.

I'd been cross-dressing for years in private, by myself or in controlled environments where I felt safe from harassment. As a child, my mum's clothes captivated me – a grey-green, heavy silk dress she'd bought in Greece, a beaded necklace from Sudan. I would steal moments alone to try these things on and would feel so alive. Fuelled by too much cider as a teenager, I would experiment with makeup and my female friends' wardrobes. At music festivals, I would show off with my clothes, yet slip by unnoticed in the crowd.

Dressing in women's clothing has always been a part of my identity, but this time the context had shifted. This wasn't a drunken game, a camp performance, or a shameful secret. It was sincere, it was open and it was vulnerable.

That first night of the show was both terrifying and liberating. But as we continued our performance across the world, it was in Leith, just outside Edinburgh in the summer of 2013 that stays with me the most.

The first day of the show I wore men's clothes, walked through a large supermarket and past a pub with a new person every 15 minutes. On one of these journeys, a man outside the pub collapsed. Instinctively I went to help him, and as I waited for an ambulance a crowd gathered. When the paramedics took over, the landlord shook my hand and told me I was a hero.

The following day, I wore a long black dress, high heels, lipstick and mascara. Having happily walked by unnoticed with my ever-changing companions, I now stuck out like a sore thumb. It was on my second trip through the supermarket that the manager called me aside. He'd received complaints about my presence in the shop, that I was "making customers and staff feel uneasy". I would not be allowed back in.

In the street outside, I was spat at, verbally abused and physically threatened. The landlord, who the day before had called me a hero, took one look and shouted, "Faggot!" I'd been used to strange looks, people taking photographs and name-calling, but nothing this hostile. I felt unlawful, immoral and unsafe. I wanted to hide, to cancel the show, go back to my bed, take off my makeup and change my clothes.

By the fifth person, I couldn't hold in my tears any longer. A friend of mine was next to walk, and I confided in him that I was thinking of cancelling the rest of the day. But as we spoke, his words filled me with confidence. I came to understand that it wasn't about me anymore, that it had never been about me. To the "uneasy" people spitting or jeering, it wasn't personal, it was political. By going against the norm I had gone from a hero to a faggot.

Whenever someone cross-dresses in *Walking:Holding,* they are now accompanied by some form of security. As I continued to walk through Leith, I thought about all the people who didn't have that protection. The people who had to 'risk assess' their lives every day. Of the young boy scolded for simple curiosity, to the trans woman murdered on the streets of Brazil. And their untold stories gave me strength to carry on walking.

I thought about the people that had walked before me. The marches I'd missed. Quentin Crisp and Marsha P. Johnson walked beside me as they had done years ago, alongside beautiful strangers from all over the world. From all over history. Not just cross-dressers, but the millions of people who had to fiercely edit themselves in order to exist without fear of persecution. And with them in my mind's eye, we walked in solidarity. With the silent acceptance that our bodies, and the way we choose to show them, have never and will never owe anybody an explanation.

31
OUT AND ABOUT
Jay Jamnadas

I always knew there was something a little different about me. I couldn't articulate what it was, but as a child it was clear that I shouldn't talk about it openly. When my teenage years came, I realised what that difference was – I liked boys, not girls. The first person I told was my best friend when we were both 15. It was such a relief to be able to tell someone, to have someone else to talk with about it.

It was at university that I really found myself. I saw that being gay was OK, and for the most part people accepted others for who they were. Quite frankly, they didn't care either way. By the time I graduated from law school, I was 'out' to all my friends and classmates. They even went with me on my first gay clubbing experience.

When I entered the corporate world, however, I decided to keep my sexuality in the closet. The message transmitted by the media and society in general was that being gay was a barrier to success. It was six months into my job that I saw this assumption challenged. My new supervisor was gay, well-respected, and on track to make partner. It was a revelation – I could be true to myself and still make it up the ranks.

Coming from a tightly knit Indian community, I knew that the reception wouldn't be so straightforward closer to home. Nobody was openly gay in my extended family or among the people whose opinions mattered most to my parents. I'd always told myself that I would only 'come out' to them once I was in a committed relationship and living a life independent of the family home. I wanted to be fully prepared for a scenario where they rejected me for my sexuality.

Although the more times I had said "I am gay" the easier it had become, the prospect of saying it to my parents brought back the same dread that I had felt the first time round. Once said, you can never take it back. On arrival at their house, it took me an hour to pluck up the courage to tell them that we needed to talk. I chose my words carefully. Instead of saying: "I have

something to tell you," implying the confession of something negative, I said: "I have something to share". That I was gay; that I had felt it since I was four; that I had known since I was 12; that I had struggled with it for all those years in between; and that being gay was who I am.

My parents took some time to come to terms with it, but they didn't reject me as I had feared. Their main concern was based on their traditional idea of happiness: a man could only be happy if he married a woman and had children – there was no other path. By inverting this winning formula, they believed I would accordingly be unhappy. They have since come to accept that this is my life, and that my partner is integral to it. He is now seen as a part of the family, just as my nephews and nieces treat him as their uncle.

I realise that I will continue to have many more 'coming out' experiences throughout my life. Not only to my friends and colleagues, but also to less intimate people like builders, doctors and call centre operators. I always correct the assumption that my partner is a 'she', because I want people to see the diversity in the world, to challenge the idea of normality.

In seeking acceptance I've become more accepting of others, and ultimately more accepting of myself. In the end, people's opinions matter less. With the support of those close to me, I've made a choice to face the world as I am.

32 THE HISTORY BOYS

Scott & David Barclay

There's a saying up here, 'people make Glasgow', and they certainly do. We had been together for 11 years at the time, in a civil partnership for seven, but it never felt the same. We were never on the same footing as our married friends. I couldn't even refer to my partner as husband. Neither could he to me.

As we now pore over the extraordinary collection of photos, greetings cards and those infamous press cuttings, we are reminded that it was all by accident really. When we booked our wedding, we had no idea we were fated to make history that day. The first clue came in the form of a phone call from one of the main news channels in Scotland asking to film us on the morning of our big day. Only then did it begin to dawn on us. Then the BBC called, then the Daily Mail, The Sun, The Mirror and publications from as far afield as Dubai and California. It went a bit crazy!

Granted, not many people have 20 photographers, a bunch of television crews and a road in Glasgow city centre shut off for the occasion, not to mention protesters. But this wasn't any wedding. We were to be the very first same sex couple to be married in Scotland, and that came with some obligatory extras.

Another couple got married under Scottish law at the Australian Consulate just before us, but we were the first in Scotland. They were legally robbed of their marriage as soon as they walked out of the embassy. That made it all the more special for us. Not out of some awful schadenfreude, but because it reminded us how lucky we were to live in a country that didn't just tolerate diversity but celebrated it.

The day itself passed by in a blur, but there were a few standout moments. As we were driven up to the registry office, locals who recognised us from the papers shouted out of car windows to wish us well. It was overwhelming. Even now, over a year since it happened, we've had to stop on occasion to do

selfies with total strangers. We were live on BBC radio as we walked up the steps of the registry office – me on one line, and a Catholic priest telling us we were an abomination on the other. But the few protesters who turned up outside quickly dispersed when they realised the wave of love and respect we were being showered with by the public.

The Chief Registrar for Glasgow led the ceremony, and the very person who helped write the new law witnessed it. As we left as an officially married couple, the Cabinet Minister who signed the act into law toasted us with a glass of champagne – he popped the cork so hard it nearly put a hole in the ceiling of the office.

As we left we were ushered through the back doors to avoid the press, only to be greeted by a crowd of photographers, television crews, and strangers who cheered our names and threw confetti. It was the most surreal moment of our lives.

One question every reporter asked us was, "Do you feel any different?" The answer is yes. It validated our relationship in a country that before had said our relationship wasn't as important as our friends' and family's. Yes, we still have the same lives. Yes, we still have to go to work and pay the same bills. But yes, we honestly feel different.

We're not saying marriage is for everyone, indeed some same sex couples don't want to get married at all. But now they have a choice. Has equality now been reached in this country? We would both unanimously say no. Equality will be reached when there is no need for all this attention, when it will just be another two people getting married regardless of genders.

To be in the history books is special; to think that in decades to come when another generation studies equality in school our names will come up. The best thing came a few months after our wedding. We were walking in a shopping centre when a man in his fifties approached us, shook our hands, and with tears in his eyes recalled how we had made it easier for his son to come out to him. He just hugged us and left. If that's our legacy, it's some legacy.

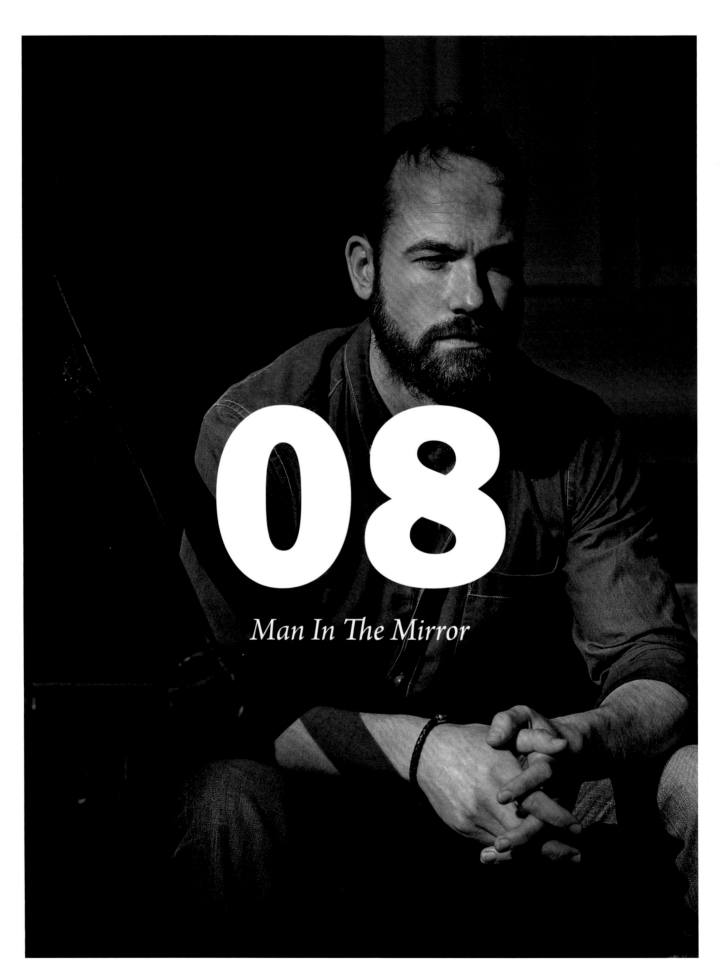

08

Man In The Mirror

33

THE BEST MEDICINE

Dave Chawner

My name's Dave, and I'm a comedian. If you haven't heard of me, don't worry… no one else has! I'm just a stand-up comic. In fact, that's what this is about. People say laughter's the best medicine. I think it's an even better antidote. Comedy has a unique way of reaching people – it makes things more engaging, less intimidating and easier to understand. Things like eating disorders.

I've had anorexia for the past ten years. I've read about people's 'journey' into eating disorders, mine was more of a diversion – a subtle detour that took me away from myself. Anorexia was something I slipped into over time. It wasn't vanity or attention seeking. It was an addiction and an obsession. It was a game I played. A game that I loved – the buzz of losing weight, restricting food and exercising; the sensation of feeling lithe, waiflike and emaciated. I loved it so much, I didn't realise I had a problem.

It all started when I was 17. I got a role in a school play. I had to appear topless, so I decided to lose some weight. As I lost weight I got compliments about my appearance. As someone who's constantly seeking approval, it was amazing. Even more amazingly, I got the attention of an incredible, funny, beautiful girl. I'd never been noticed by girls before. We started dating and I fell in love. I was incredibly happy with how things were.

Unfortunately that happiness had a time limit. University was just around the corner; I'd be moving away from my friends, family and loving girlfriend. That scared me. I wanted to stop time, hold everything just how it was. But I couldn't.

Anorexia became a subliminal response to my situation. It seemed that when I'd begun to lose weight everything had changed for the better – I'd found my girlfriend, felt comfortable in myself and stable in my life. So, it seemed rational that the more weight I lost the better things would get.

Anorexia became a distraction. It was something above the day-to-day trappings of life that were intimidating me so much. I had UCAS applications, essay deadlines, exams, coursework, and all the insecurities any teenager has. Everything was overwhelming. If I could focus on restricting calories and obsess about how much I exercised, then it was something else to concentrate on and became a place I could hide.

Over time it became my normality, always playing in the background. I was so caught up in it I couldn't see what was going on. It's hard to tell when a social drinker becomes an alcoholic. It's the same with eating disorders. It took me eight years before I sought help. By then anorexia had become a part of my identity.

When you stop feeding your body, you stop nourishing your mind. Without fuel your brain can't release the chemicals it needs. That has an impact on your mood and I became depressed. I'd always assumed people with depression knew they were depressed. I didn't. I was too close to my own life to gain that perspective. It was like trying to look at a huge painting while only inches away from it. Slowly I became

numb to everything. So I hid. I stopped replying to messages, texts and emails. Even if I wanted to talk, what would I say?

On 11th August last year Robin Williams took his own life. It shocked me. It began to dawn how long I'd been consistently feeling this way. I'd been waiting for something to break. Reading the news of his death made me realise where that can lead you.

I plucked up the courage to go to the GP. They diagnosed me as severely clinically anorexic. I was put on immediate treatment and began an intensive course of therapy. 16 months later, it's really helped me get back on track. After all, the brain's just another part of your body – you're bound to get a few injuries along the way.

We've all got our own shit in life, no one escapes unscathed. But if you can acknowledge your differences, accept them and make them your own, that's where identity begins. We all have that potential. So, in our own individual ways we are all normally abnormal.

34
AN ACT IN VEIN
Ian Wales

I followed my dad's example of giving blood the moment I was old enough to start donating myself. On one occasion, the nurse handed me a leaflet about bone marrow and asked if I wanted to sign up. At the time, it seemed as though finding a donor-recipient match was so unlikely that the only effort required on my part was to fill in the form. So I did, and thought no more about it.

Four years later, when I was in my final year at university, I got a phone call. Was I fit and well? Still interested in becoming a donor? Could I take some blood tests? I was a match for somebody who needed a transplant. Within a couple of days I had passed the tests and was asked to come to Bristol for the operation. The timing was a bit inconvenient – I had to miss a skiing holiday planned with my friends. But as it happened, the extra free time was well used studying for a resit exam. Over the following few weeks, I gave two pints of blood that would be given back to me during the procedure, and I busied myself taking iron tablets and eating liver and bacon in preparation.

It was only when I had been flown down to Bristol that it occurred to me that there was more to this than a blood donation. The day before the operation a doctor showed me the needle that would be used. I say needle, my memory is of something between a knitting needle and a sword. He explained how I would lie face down under general anaesthetic, while two people rummaged around in my pelvic bone to suck out a litre and a half of lumpy, marrow-rich blood.

Poorly-informed horror stories started to play on my imagination. Never mind the recipient, I became convinced that I would need a walking stick for life myself.

The first thing I remember of the procedure was being rudely awoken by a suppository. The operation was a success, and by the evening I was enjoying Beef Wellington at home with my family.

Due to the amount of blood taken during the operations, it took a week for the tiredness to wear off. But I was a student; I was used to lazing around. Back at university, friends repeated what a good deed it was. However, I didn't really feel I'd done very much. It hadn't cost me anything, in fact it saved me the cost of a skiing holiday. I felt like a bit of a fraud, until the guilt gradually diminished alongside the praise, and it was all practically forgotten.

Forgotten, that is, until a couple of years later when I received a letter. The envelope was franked with the National Blood Service stamp and the contents were handwritten. Parts had been blanked out to preserve anonymity, but he explained that he was in remission and how grateful he was for the extra time he'd been given with his wife and daughter. I don't know why but I cried. I'd barely thought about him until then.

Until that point, I hadn't given my recipient a personality. The donation process is designed to be anonymous to remove feelings in case the operation is unsuccessful. Or maybe in case it is successful – there should be no obligation in either direction. I contented myself knowing that I might never know the outcome.

Even now, when I think about giving bone marrow there's a pain in my throat, and I want to say thank you to him. Not for the compliments or the special treatment I received, but for giving me the chance to help someone in need. In the end, he didn't know it, but he did me a favour too. The degree I received after my resit was just on the right side of a borderline 2:1. Who knows what a ski trip might have done to tip the balance.

35 A GLASS HALF FULL
Richard W H Bray

I t started as an itch on my spine, just on the right side, by the final rib. It was a December morning between Christmas and New Year that I noticed. I'd flipped my mattress the night before and thought at first that I'd slept wrong, that I'd pinched a nerve. It was awkward to reach, but when I ran my fingers over the spot it was quickly apparent that there was nothing on the skin. It was deeper.

I ignored it at first. Then the sensation began to spread. It became difficult to work out where it was and where it wasn't. I stayed away from the internet. I thought, doctor first, then internet. When I went to my GP they poked and prodded my limbs to test my responses, and arranged for me to meet a neurologist.

The neurologist was dry and Irish. By then my symptoms covered most of my right side and my feet were numb. I asked what it might be, and he was curt and honest. His response petrified me. "It might be MS," he said, as though it was the most normal diagnosis in the book. I felt my world change.

After an awkward MRI with my jeans around my ankles and an excruciating lumbar puncture, the evidence was conclusive. I had Multiple Sclerosis. I was only familiar with the version of the disease whose diagnosis came with a wheelchair and a speedy decay. That night I stayed up with a bottle of whisky until sunrise. At five in the morning I raised a glass to watch through the amber liquid as our nearest star lifted slowly above the sea on the horizon. I felt I should shed a tear, but couldn't.

I ran 35 miles a week. I had written a book and was writing another. I made wine, and started a new job. Something inside me wanted to ruin all of that. My own immune system had turned against me. But there was more than that. This could be my out, my excuse to just give in. Who could blame me? No. I couldn't let this change who I was. It might cut a huge swathe of my life, but not me. Between me, the North Sea and the rising sun behind it, I decided that no matter what happened I would not allow something that was taking my life to ruin my life.

36 BAG FOR LIFE
Ed Corrie

I was diagnosed with Crohn's disease when I was 14. I had been losing weight for months and was crippled with stomach cramps. Barely able to eat, what I could manage just ran straight through me. And then there was the blood. Lots of blood.

Crohn's is an inflammatory bowel disease that affects around one person in every thousand. The lining of the gastrointestinal tract becomes inflamed and ulcerated, and ceases to reabsorb fluids through the bowel wall. The peristalsis means that anything moving over the infected area causes it to bleed constantly, like perpetually reopening a graze on your knee.

School life can be a tough existence at the best of times. Playground politics are fickle and cruel – I remember folks in my year getting nicknames based on total lies, but they stuck, even to this day. Couple this with a time when you're starting to think about sex and relationships, and you're in a pretty vulnerable position. To be the guy with the aggressive shitting problem, who has to go to the bathroom every two minutes, is not something you'd want your peers finding out about. That kind of thing could destroy you. So I kept a lid on it. At friends' houses or on school trips – whenever I had to share rooms with randoms – I monopolised the toilet. I would pretend that I had a vomiting problem, somehow that was more acceptable. More manly.

So when I had to have my large intestine removed and woke up with a colostomy bag, I suppose I was ready for it, even though it came as a shock. Even though I was waking up to the nightmare that had haunted me throughout my teenage years. You see, in all this time I was proud that I never once used Crohn's as an excuse or reason not to do something. It was inside me, hidden. But now, aged 20 my physiology was different somehow, and it was unknown, scary territory. I was a guy with a bag, and for the first time ever this illness was going to define me.

So I let it define me. But on my terms.

After spending a day crying from the initial shock, I vowed never to cry over it again. My parents had been crippled by the anxiety at the prospect of the several operations I would have to endure, and I needed to be strong for them. I was also in danger of being kicked out of university if I took more than three weeks off, so I made it my mission to get out of hospital and back on campus in time to finish my degree.

An altercation with a horrific nurse spurred me on. She had final say over whether I was mentally strong enough to leave hospital, which pushed me to prove her wrong. I got up every morning, early. I showered and dressed in my regular clothes (no pyjamas, no hospital gowns) and I would exercise gently by walking around the hospital.

But I had more than just that to get me back on my feet. Before I woke up with the bag, I was under the impression that I was about to die. Waking up at all seemed an unexpected bonus, and now I try to make the most of every day that has followed since.

I won't lie and say that it was easy, with me skipping around high-fiving everyone. There were hard, dark days in there. But being surrounded by friends, family and loved ones, with healthy, positive focuses really helped me get through it. When I had the bag, I even met a girl who taught me to laugh at it and to feel human again. That wouldn't have happened had I been wallowing in self-pity, angry at the world.

Sometimes we get dealt a shitty hand in life – in my case, almost literally – but by taking the right attitude it can define you for the right reasons. It could always be a lot worse.

09

Men are from Venus

37 CALL THE MIDWIFE
Richard Magondu

Like other parts of the world, midwifery in Kenya is closely associated with women, but this ideology is progressively shifting.

After finishing my high school studies, I was presented with the option of two career courses – one in Sports Management, the other in Nursing and Midwifery. The answer was clear. Growing up, I knew that I wanted to work with people in a caring environment. Midwifery seemed the perfect fit. I trained as a Registered Nurse Midwife at the Medical Training College in Nyeri, and have been practising ever since.

For five years I have worked in the maternity department for one of the busiest hospitals in Kenya. In this time I have conducted over 3,000 deliveries, yet I still get the same feeling of delight after every single birth.

Challenges are never far away in maternity. The most painful moments for me are when we lose a woman during delivery. There is always that feeling that I could have done something to save her life, and no matter how many deaths you witness, you're never quite ready for the next one. The best moment is a few minutes after birth, when I get to unite the newborn baby with its mother. It is so satisfying to see her happy and smiling after hours of anguish in labour, especially for new mothers.

On 2nd February 2008, I was able to experience my job from the other side of the screen. My daughter was due to be born, and I had the privilege of conducting her delivery. I was on day duty when my now wife called to inform me she was experiencing pains. A colleague covered for me while I rushed some 100 kilometres, excited about the prospect of accomplishing my lifelong dream. The on-call midwife was gracious enough to allow me to attend to her in labour, and my daughter was born five minutes before midnight. Holding the tiny thing in my arms felt incredible, every fibre of my body tickled with levity. Delivering a baby must be one of the major life privileges a man can ever experience.

38 LOVE IS IN THE HAIR

Nonni Quest

I never wanted to become a hairdresser. My mum's a hairdresser, my grandmother an aesthetician, and my father has imported hair products since I was a kid. I grew up surrounded by other hairdressers in a hair salon, breathing in hair product fumes. I'd had enough.

School life wasn't for me. I couldn't wait to leave. Not knowing which direction to take, I followed my friends to study business, but royally failed the first semester. I had worked in the family salon that Christmas, and hairdressing no longer seemed a course I could avoid. A brief trip to the guidance counsellor confirmed as much. So it was that I trained to be a barber.

It's funny how we sometimes look for our passion in the most distant places, when they're actually standing right in front of us the whole time. I've had opportunities along the way that would have been easy to pass by, but I have always taken on the challenge. I've worked for international companies, and had the chance to travel and live in Russia for two years. I've worked for the media, held fashion shows and seminars, and eventually opened my own salon. That was 17 years ago, and I've been running it ever since. Sticking to my profession has been a great investment in experience and knowledge. Every time I get tired of my work, which happens to us all every now and then, I always try to reinvent myself within my craft to gain a new advantage.

Beta and I met in 2004. At the time, she was the manager of a cosmetics company in Iceland and I was running my family's salon. We often talked about having a place where we could unite all of our interests together and create a multifunctional operation. Before we knew it, we were working together. There was no strategy, it just happened. Beta is the most positive person I know. She has a brilliant marketing mind, she's solutions-orientated, and most of all is great with people. She really helps lift me off the pragmatic ground I tend to get stuck on, while I keep her tethered so she won't drift too far away. In 2011, our multifunctional business started for real. Today

we own and run a place called Quest – Hair, Beer & Whisky Saloon, the first and only liquor licensed hair salon in Iceland. In this place we simply do exactly what we want. In the daytime I cut hair while Beta runs our wholesale distribution business, and in the evenings we host exclusive whisky and beer tastings, concerts, art exhibitions and poetry evenings. It's a lot of work, and holidays come few and far between. But if you spend all of your time with the people you love, doing what you love, isn't life just one big holiday?

In the end, my place is at home. I feel a great sense of belonging in my small community, in my small city, on my small island of Iceland. Today we have a small family of our own – two boys, Jón Tumi and Ingimundur Emil. There is so much love under one roof. In the end, it all comes down to the people. You can't do much without people.

39 A NEW LIFE IS BORN

Jack Morris

My single biggest tip for any expectant, first-time father would be this – expect the unexpected. Hey, expect the expected too.

Aged 28, and a newly married man, I walked out of my job and found myself unemployed for the first time in my adult life. It wasn't just any job either. I was a Police Officer of seven years, a 'job for life' as society would have you believe. Well paid, respected (depending on who you're talking to), a career to make your parents proud and impress new in-laws.

The general response was, "You're going to be a stay-at-home dad, that's cool, lots of guys do that these days". Just one slight problem there. When I left work I didn't have any children, and we weren't expecting any either. I was simply a stay-at-home man.

So what does a stay-at-home man do? Well, the same things a housewife does, I guess. The dynamic of our relationship has always been that I do all the cooking, and I don't think my wife would put up any argument if I said that this is because I'm much better at it. The commitments imposed by my wife's work means she is glad to have me there each evening, rather than coming home at all hours, sometimes not coming home at all. I bake, I clean, I organise house affairs, budgets and bills. I have dinner ready for her return every day, and I clean up afterwards. I'm a support network of one.

Do I feel any less masculine because of this? Not in the slightest. To say men can't look after the home for the good of their family would be as narrow-minded as saying women shouldn't be offered the same opportunities as men in the workplace.

A rather gross selfie taken six months into our marriage, complete with pee-covered stick, marked the second pregnancy test of that week. This was due to a very rare occurrence in our relationship – I was actually right about something. Despite having all the symptoms, my wife had ignored the instructions

on what stage of the cycle to take the test, and our first result had been negative. Never argue with a guy about a battery-operated gadget. One point to me.

I spent the whole morning being unnecessarily cautious and caring, peaking a little too soon as the supportive husband considering the nine months ahead. That afternoon I went out to buy vitamins, decaf tea and coffee, and ordered a pregnancy bible on the internet. Sadly, it turned out my wife doesn't like decaf tea or coffee, so I'm still gradually playing Tea Roulette with myself until they're gone.

Four months in, and our little sprout was growing well. As an ex-cop I've seen it all when it comes to bodily fluids, and have had most of them on me at one time or another. I liked to think I was pretty well set for it, and in some ways I was. Watching my wife suffer morning sickness at point blank range was no issue, but the emotional drain was huge.

Despite my protests, we didn't discover the gender. When we had our first scan, my wife refused to find out. She wanted something to push for. My one and only window of opportunity for the next 20 weeks had just sailed on by like Halley's Comet. I always thought that deep down every man must want a son. A little boy to do boyish things with, like build forts and climb trees and go camping. A little version of themselves. But then girls can build forts, and climb trees, and go camping too. Especially if she was my girl. I had learned enough from my own experience not to put our child in a box.

In July 2015 I was officially promoted from stay-at-home man to stay-at-home dad. It took 26 hours from contractions in a restaurant, to our son Toby taking his first breath. And there our next little adventure began.

My wife runs a successful business and has a baby – some might say she has it all. But does that then suggest I have nothing? My wife is the perfect mum, and our home life strikes the perfect balance. Having it all, it turns out, is all about what makes you happy… and we couldn't be happier.

40
SOMETHING OLD SOMETHING NEW

Dave Kirk

Looking back, our friends all said that we were meant to be. Perhaps they were right. I first met Tamara in the summer of 2000 at the end of our first year in sixth form, since we had both applied to read Theology at the same Oxford college. Tamara was applying because she was already very academic and hardworking, and I was applying because one of my teachers told me not to bother, I'd never get in. Big mistake. That was the greatest motivator I could have been given.

We were both outgoing and made a connection almost immediately. Although we were quietly a bit stressed by the whole thing, we decided to go out for a few drinks together to relax while the more bookish applicants revised deep into the night, getting more and more fraught. We got on amazingly well over those two or three days, and even though I had a girlfriend at the time, we both sensed that somehow we would play an important part in each other's lives in the years to come.

Having exchanged emails, we were delighted to be able to celebrate together when we both received written offers from Lady Margaret Hall. While it was a daunting prospect to study at Oxford, alongside all those intimidatingly clever people, it was great to know that I would have a friend to see on my first day there.

Lo and behold, we got on like a house on fire throughout our undergraduate years, whether it was going to lectures, clubs, college parties, the Bodleian library, or for our customary pint at the Rose and Crown. Tamara even helped convince me not to give up after the first year when I was struggling with a tough workload coupled with my parents' divorce. Everything in my life as I know it now would have turned out differently without her, and without her good advice.

It wasn't until a year or so after university that things started to change for us. I decided to continue my studies in Edinburgh, while Tamara went to take her teaching PGCE back home in

Lancashire. We had both just come out of difficult relationships, and she invited me to a party back home. The trouble was, her ex-boyfriend was holding one the same weekend, and most of our mutual friends ended up going to that. Suddenly it was just me going to her party alone. When I arrived, the big meal she had planned at an Italian restaurant turned into a candlelit dinner for two. She was so beautiful that night, and one of my very best friends. I remember being caught out by the sudden change in chemistry. That was the pivotal moment for our relationship.

Soon after we started seeing each other properly, we fell in love. On completing our studies, we moved south – Tamara to Hertfordshire for her first teaching position, and me to London to start my career in coins and military medals. After some years spent seeing each other on weekends, we moved in together in Barnet. It was on a return visit to Edinburgh for the New Year in 2012 that I proposed during a sunny afternoon on Calton Hill. By the summer of 2014 we were married at our old college in Oxford by one of the very people who had first interviewed us 14 years earlier. It was a beautiful, fairytale English wedding, and I just remember having a huge, beaming smile as I saw her walk down the aisle of the college chapel, without a single doubt in my mind that this was the woman I wanted to marry, to love, and to spend my life with.

Too often in our modern western culture we are told to fear commitment – that being single is the greatest time of your life, that marriage is the end of freedom, and that from then on you are tied down by the ball and chain. But I don't see it like that. Marriage settles things, and in a good way. I'm not a perfect person, far from it, but I have taken Christian vows that I am proud of, made in front of God, my family and my peers, and I know that I have been blessed to meet and fall in love with this incredible person. We have so much fun together, and sometimes the little things are the most special. Memories shared from university, from our honeymoon, silly moments or conversations, watching TV, waking up together, and the comfort of always knowing that I live with a smart, beautiful woman, who just happens to be my best friend. Naturally she drives me mad sometimes, she's not always the tidiest, and despite having two degrees she still doesn't remember to turn the lights off in the spare room… but there's always room for improvement! In return, I'm still figuring out how not to shrink all her dresses and cashmere jumpers.

We challenge each other intellectually, and that's not always easy, but we approach our relationship with humour, love and mutual respect. Having been friends first, we always have that connection on which everything else is built. Even though we lead busy lives, we try hard to make our marriage work and do special things together, just for us. On the other hand, we've already worked through some hard challenges, but with talking and keeping an open heart you work it out. It's great to know that someone totally has your back.

Marriage takes patience and compromise, but it's the greatest thing I ever did.

ACKNOWLEDGEMENTS

PHOTO CREDITS

Cover photo and majority of photos within the book by Priya Dabasia, *Being ManKind Ltd*

Additional photos supplied by:
LEON NEAL/AFP/Getty Images, p8
Roland Lane, Men's Fitness, p15, p17
Chris Parkes, p21
Mark Pollock Trust, p23-25
Michael Wharley Photography, p31
Virgin Unite, p53
Beautiful Bairns Photography, p71
Richard Davenport, p109-111
Jose Reyes, p151
Neha Shah, p161

LOCATION CREDITS FOR PHOTOS

Stopgap Dance Company, Surrey
Clime-it Brothers, Camden
Mr Bao, Peckham
Aspect Studios, Loughborough
Tom Chapman hair design, Torquay
Peckham BMX Club, London
The Roundhouse, Camden
Events hosted by Amazonas Arts, Brighton and Bemvindo Capoeira, London
Milk Cafe, Glasgow
Village Hotel, Glasgow
Quest - Hair, Beer & Whisky saloon, Reykjavik, Iceland

THANKS TO

We are overwhelmed by the support we have received for this project. We would like to acknowledge, with much appreciation, the people listed below for their contribution to the project, ranging from helping to source stories to providing invaluable advice *(in alphabetical order)*:

Ambica Jobanputra

Amy Davies Dolamore (Bryony Kimmings Ltd)

Anthony Brandon Bravo

Anusha Kumar

Beckie Smith (Red Sky Management)

Bill Bateman

Bipin Sanghrajka

Cameron Shields

Cherie Brennan & Lucy Bennett (Stopgap Dance Company)

Chris Elliott

Claire Grant

Craig McGinlay

Dave Rogers

David Brockway (The Great Initiative)

David Edgar

Deep Sanghrajka

Dylan Roberts

Dyno Keatinge

Elodie Draperi

Emily Churchill Zaraa

Eva Philippaki

Fred Bateman

Graham Martin

Hanna Gillespie-Gallery

Harry Watkins

Hesham Abaumer

Hugo Mitchell

Ian Richardson

Jane Boyle

Jason Wisdom

John Adams

John Holland

Jon Lipsey (Alpha Man Magazine)

Jonathan Shannon (Coach Magazine)

Jude Edgar

Kamini Patel

Konnaire Scannell

Leslee Udwin

Luisa Omielan

Matt Clarke

Michael Gonedro

Nicola Finnigan (Village Hotel, Glasgow)

Nishma Jethwa

Paul Dean

Purnima Sanghrajka

Richard Woods

Rob West

Ruth Watkins

Sarah O'Donovan (Mark Pollock Trust)

Sonal Sachdev Patel

Stefan Moghina

Stuart Brundritt

Stuart John

Suvi Dogra

Tara Keatinge

Theo Philippakis

Theresa McCabe

Tony Jameson-Allen

Tor Evans (The Roundhouse, Camden)

Zoe Marriage

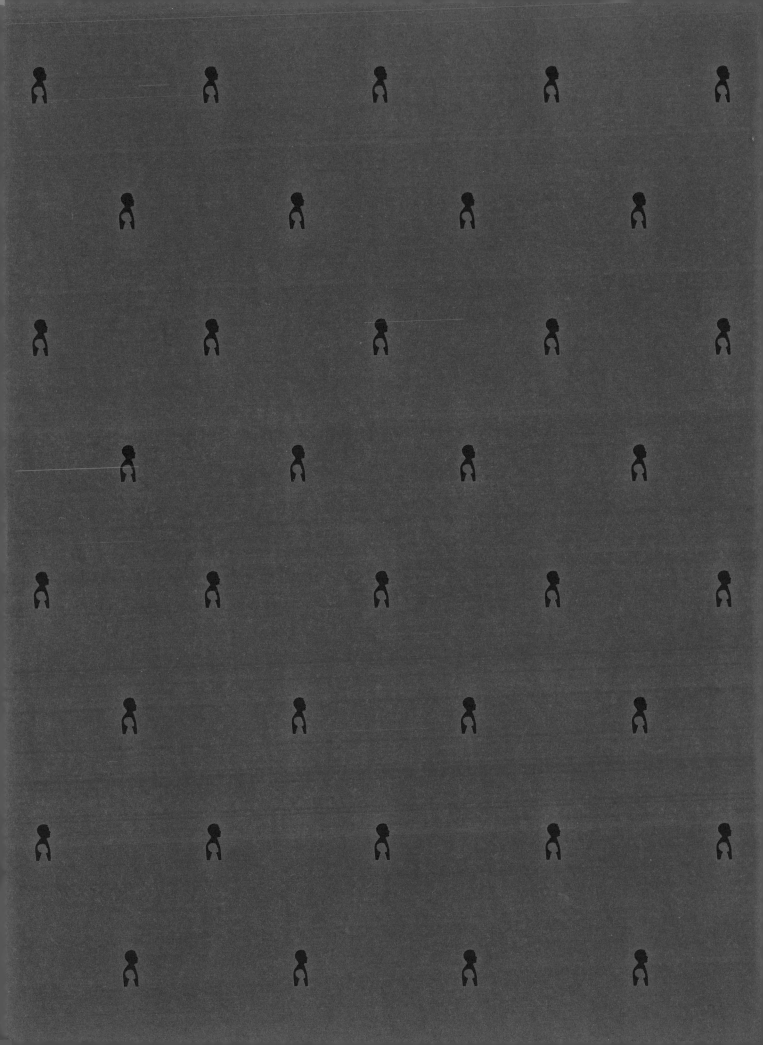